DARIO FO
ABDUCTING DIANA
(Il ratto della Francesca)

ADAPTED BY STEPHEN STENNING
From a translation by Rupert Lowe

Oberon Books

London

This translation/adaptation first published in Great Britain in 1994 by Oberon Books Limited, 521 Caledonian Road, London N7 9RH. Tel: 071 607 3637/Fax: 071 607 3629

Printed by Multiplex Medway Ltd.

ISBN 1 870259 45 9

Cover design: Andrzej Klimowski

OBERON BOOKS
521 Caledonian Road
London N7 9RH
Tel: 071 607 3637

This adaptation of *Abducting Diana* was first performed at the Pleasance Theatre on 10 August, 1994, during the Edinburgh International Fringe Festival, presented by Warrick Producing Consultants in a Moving Theatre production, with the following production team and cast:

DIANA, Susan Penhaligon
YOUNG MAN, Richard Brightiff
CHIEF KIDNAPPER, Ray Boot
KIDNAPPER 2, Benedict Taylor
KIDNAPPER 3, Robert McCulley
MOTHER, Clare Welch
PRIEST, Ron Welling

Director: Jonathan Banatvala
Designer: Alistair Livingstone
Lighting: Christopher Corner
Executive producer: Christopher Warrick

Note on the adaptation

Il ratto della Francesca (The kidnapping of Francesca) was first performed in 1986. This is the first English adaptation. The political satire in the original was aimed at contemporary Italian politicians, caricatured by the masks the kidnappers wore. None of the politicians were representative of any political movement or party in Italy, but were ridiculed for their appearance, idiosyncrasies and public image. More than other Fo plays, *Il ratto della Francesca* relies on topical observations. This adaptation is not as dependent on topicality, yet it requires a degree of news value that can only be hinted at in a published script.

The character of Francesca was a banker. Dario Fo's original looked at the relationship between bankers and politicians, questioning the relationship. How corrupt is it? Who controls who? In this version, Diana is a media magnate. Are politicians ruled by the media? Or vice versa? Who manages the news we receive and for what purpose? The open political ambitions of those who own the media are obvious, the recent striking example being Silvio Berlusconi, Italian Prime Minister and media boss.

CHARACTERS

WOMAN/DIANA FORBES-MCKAYE
YOUNG MAN
CHIEF KIDNAPPER
KIDNAPPER 2
KIDNAPPER 3
MOTHER
PRIEST

ACT ONE

SCENE 1

[*Lights up on a City apartment with one large window, with a blind that is pulled up. All the furniture is covered with dust-sheets and the room clearly does not get regular use. There is however a large sofa-bed in the centre of the room*]

[*WOMAN enters dragging YOUNG MAN who is blindfolded and has his hands tied*]

WOMAN: Come along! This way! [*Going to window but making sure she can't be seen from outside*]

YOUNG MAN: Ouch!

WOMAN: Keep close, then you won't walk in to the furniture. Now come here! Get your head down there. [*Forces head down below level of window*]

YOUNG MAN: Already! Can't we chat a bit first... Maybe kiss or... I'm not used...

WOMAN: Shhh! Keep away from the window while I draw the blinds. [*Does so*]

YOUNG MAN: Mrs McKaye?...

WOMAN: You may call me Diana now.

YOUNG MAN: Diana, at lunch you said you'd give me some tips for my career... Why am I blindfolded?

WOMAN: [*Looking carefully through the blinds*] I don't want us to be spied on from outside. [*Leads him to sofa*] Come over here! Sit down!

YOUNG MAN: So you're ashamed of me!

WOMAN: First tip; As chief executive of a television station and owner of three national newspapers, I'm obliged to justify media intrusions into people's private lives. It is therefore essential to keep the grubbier side of my own life secret.

YOUNG MAN: I see!

WOMAN: As a spotty office worker from Romford, you are that grubbier side.

YOUNG MAN: Hornchurch! I haven't got spots!

WOMAN: Well, Kevin from Hornchurch this is your big chance.

YOUNG MAN: My name's not Kevin.

WOMAN: Have you a health certificate?

YOUNG MAN: I'm sorry?

WOMAN: A certificate to prove your... healthy.

YOUNG MAN: I doubt it; can't even find my medical card.

WOMAN: Right then, before we get down to it, a little preparation... [*Gets out medical set and syringe*]

YOUNG MAN: Foreplay?

WOMAN: Yes if you like, sort of... I'll untie your hands! This won't hurt! Imagine I'm a nurse and you're the patient.

YOUNG MAN: Ahh right! You're wearing one of those uniforms with black stockings a suspender belt and...

WOMAN: You don't waste your train journeys on the FT. [*Preparing the syringe*] How are your glands?

YOUNG MAN: What glands?

WOMAN: In your neck - any swellings?

YOUNG MAN: Not in my neck. [*Giggles*]

WOMAN: Under the armpits? [*Checks*]

YOUNG MAN: [*Giggling*] That tickles!

WOMAN: Stick out your tongue. Show me your gums. Any diarrhoea?

YOUNG MAN: [*Still giggling*] In my gums?

WOMAN: [*Doing it*] Roll up the sleeves.

YOUNG MAN: [*Still giggling*] It tickles.

WOMAN: Hold still.

YOUNG MAN: Ow! Shit! You've punctured me.

WOMAN: Just a little prick!

YOUNG MAN: What!

WOMAN: A blood sample.

YOUNG MAN: A blood sample.

WOMAN: Not conclusive, of course, but it reassures.

YOUNG MAN: You're off your trolley.

WOMAN: Just cautious - I need to check this. [*Takes a chart from bag*]

YOUNG MAN: What's going on?

WOMAN: Calm down! [*Checking colour against a chart*] That looks fine. Nothing to worry about.

YOUNG MAN: You're mad!

WOMAN: Not at all. As our government is unwilling to bring in mandatory certificates, the responsibility lies with the sexually active individual. Glass of mineral water?

YOUNG MAN: Completely barking mad.

WOMAN: It isn't a thorough safeguard and I'll have to insist on protection for anything penetrative. You're suitably prepared?

YOUNG MAN: It's the in-breeding.

WOMAN: Do you have any condoms?

YOUNG MAN: They make nasty rings in your wallet.

WOMAN: I might have some in the bathroom. [*Enters bathroom*]

YOUNG MAN: [*Calling*] You're ruthless.

WOMAN: Thank you.

YOUNG MAN: This is your meat shop, isn't it?

WOMAN: Yes!

YOUNG MAN: Know what they call you behind your back? Fuck and chuck McKaye.

WOMAN: [*Re-entering in dressing-gown*] Not always behind my back. [*Holds up assortment of condoms*] Voila! Orange, lemon, black currant.

YOUNG MAN: Any cold beer?

WOMAN: The condoms. [*Sits beside him loosens tie and starts kissing his neck*] . Oh you've got lovely soft skin.

YOUNG MAN: Don't you feel guilty... you know... about picking me up and all that?

WOMAN: Tortured!

YOUNG MAN: Your papers expose other people's doings as guardians of the nation's morals. Then, at the first opportunity you're committing depraved acts with...

WOMAN: What depraved acts?

YOUNG MAN: Well I thought...

WOMAN: You're a very sick young man! [*Starts undoing his shirt*] And misinformed. I am a business woman, an executive, an owner. I do not write the stories nor do the snooping. Whilst on the subject, we in the media don't pass judgment, we merely reflect the attitudes of ordinary people. We don't make the news we just report, we don't have any power we just respond to the whims of society.
[*She takes off the shirt and kisses his chest*]

[*YOUNG MAN wails with passion*]

The more boring people's lives, the more they enjoy building up the lives of others. The more they then enjoy it when they're shot down. It excites them. [*Kisses his chest again*]

YOUNG MAN: Mmmmmm!

WOMAN: The public are repressed! Take away their jobs, their livelihoods, their homes - they don't know how to react. Marching, and protesting just aren't British. So we provide a release. Satan worshippers, petty bureaucrats and sex scandals. Good old fashioned reactionary fervour.

[*She goes to undo his trousers*]

YOUNG MAN: Shouldn't I be writing this down? Learning something?

WOMAN: You will, if you shut up!

YOUNG MAN: But... I thought that you... liked me... wanted to get to know me. Maybe we'd relax together, find each other...

WOMAN: Kevin! Stop trying to be a new man and get your kegs off!

[*She whips off his trousers and jumps on him*]

YOUNG MAN: You don't even know my name.

WOMAN: Who cares, kiss me.

[*They kiss. She takes off his blindfold. They embrace*]

YOUNG MAN: Coo! You've a wonderfully strong grip.

[*Phone rings*]

WOMAN: [*Suddenly sitting up*] Oh my god!

YOUNG MAN: [*Pulling her back down*] It's only the phone. Leave it!

WOMAN: [*Sitting up*] But nobody knows this number.

YOUNG MAN: [*Pulling her back down*] So? It's a wrong number.

WOMAN: You answer it. Go on!

YOUNG MAN: [*Grabs phone*] Yes?...Who?... No this is not the fire brigade! What?... Oh I'm sorry, you're the Fire Brigade... No, no one's on fire here... Of course I'm sure. Goodbye. See - wrong number.

WOMAN: Come 'ere sexy. [*They go back to embrace*]

YOUNG MAN: You're the most exciting woman...

WOMAN: So! You want to learn something? [*Goes to remove skirt*]

YOUNG MAN: Teach me! Teach me!

WOMAN: What's that?

YOUNG MAN: What?

WOMAN: [*Getting up*] I can smell burning.

YOUNG MAN: Shit! [*Aside*] Not now!

WOMAN: Smoke! From under the door! It smells like joss sticks. [*Sniffs*] Jasmine.

YOUNG MAN: Might be a fire.

WOMAN: It might be a trick.

[*The phone rings again*]

WOMAN: See!

YOUNG MAN: The phone.

WOMAN: Answer it.

YOUNG MAN: Hullo yes? What do you mean who am I? Who are you? And you!

WOMAN: Who was it?

YOUNG MAN: She didn't say.

WOMAN: She? A woman?

YOUNG MAN: She called me a deceiving bitch.

WOMAN: Not you. Me!

YOUNG MAN: That explains it.

WOMAN: She's found out! [*Goes into bathroom to find blouse*]

YOUNG MAN: Who has?

WOMAN: The boss.

YOUNG MAN: What boss?

WOMAN: She'll kill me.

YOUNG MAN: Who will?

WOMAN: [*Re-entering*] Diana Forbes-McKaye. She'll be here soon. Hurry up and get dressed.

YOUNG MAN: But you're Diana McKaye.

WOMAN: No half wit I'm not. I'm her double! Here! [*Throws him shirt*] Put it on.

YOUNG MAN: You having me on?

WOMAN: Not any more.

YOUNG MAN: [*They start dressing*] You look like McKaye.

WOMAN: I bloody well ought to. Three years in drama school. I've got her hair style, clothes, glasses and I'm in her meat-shop. Christ, she knows I've been here, she'll kill me.

YOUNG MAN: Tart!

WOMAN: It's all different now isn't it? I was an exciting woman when I had all those millions coming out of my knickers. Now I'm a tart. Where are your trousers?

YOUNG MAN: All this to knock off an actress.

WOMAN: Bastard! [*Throws him his trousers*] Trousers!

YOUNG MAN: I was going to tell the lads I'd poked McKaye.

WOMAN: Sexist lout! I preferred the New Man.

YOUNG MAN: You are really McKaye, aren't you?

WOMAN: No! She wouldn't touch an ignorant, white sock with black slip-on wearing, would-be toy-boy from Romford with an extended barge-pole.

YOUNG MAN: Hornchurch! Smoke's getting worse.

[*A siren from outside. YOUNG MAN goes to window*]

WOMAN: Get away from that window! I'll look. Turn round. [*Lifts blinds*] Firemen!

YOUNG MAN: Ah so it wasn't the wrong number.

WOMAN: How did they know about...? [*Looks again*] A grey Ford Transit? He's climbing up a wooden ladder holding a garden hose.

YOUNG MAN: Look at all that smoke.

[*Knocking at door*]

VOICE: Fire brigade! Open up! The building's going up in flames.

YOUNG MAN: Quick the key!

WOMAN: Work it out Einstein, they're not real firemen.

YOUNG MAN: Look McKaye - or whoever you are - I've been pissed around enough by you and I'm not going to fry in here.

[*She grabs key, opens door, and in clouds of smoke, two firemen burst in banging door into YOUNG MAN's face. He is knocked over*]

FIREMAN 1: Quick get out of here.

YOUNG MAN: Ow! You've broken my nose.

FIREMAN 2: [*Handing him World War II gas mask*] Put this on.

FIREMAN 1: [*Offering WOMAN mask*] Here's yours!

WOMAN: I can't. I've got a cold.

[*YOUNG MAN stands up and immediately collapses*]

FIREMAN 1: [*To FIREMAN 2*] Wrong mask, you cretin.

WOMAN: What's happened to him?

FIREMAN 1: Er... a slight bang on the cranium.

WOMAN: [*She bends over YOUNG MAN & takes off mask*] He's unconscious!

FIREMAN 2: [*Replaces mask*] He's fine!

FIREMAN 1: Come along. Quick! You better come with us. [*Grabs WOMAN. To FIREMAN 2*] Well don't just stand there, help! [*They struggle. She bites one, knees the other in the groin*]

FIREMAN 1: Owwwww!

FIREMAN 2: Ouch! She bit me!

WOMAN: [*Grabbing nail-shooter from desk*] Stay where you are.

FIREMAN 2: Put down the drill, there's a nice lady.

WOMAN: It's a high-powered repeat-action nail-shooter.

FIREMAN 2: Jesus!

WOMAN: Both of you up against the wall. [*To FIREMAN 1*] Stand up straight!

FIREMAN 1: I'm trying.

WOMAN: One false move and it's an automatic crucifixion. War-time gas-masks and a transit van - it might fool The Romford Gigolo but... [*Pointing to YOUNG MAN*] Take his mask off. Let's have a look at your faces. Off with the antiques.

FIREMAN 2: We can't... that is, it's stuck... Look!

WOMAN: [*To YOUNG MAN*] Get up and give me a hand?! [*Kicks him*]

YOUNG MAN: Aaah fan-tas-tic, huuh, I'm spent!

WOMAN: Oh my God! Well maybe this'll soften you up a bit. [*Takes fire extinguisher and starts spraying them. A third Fireman dashes in through the window and grabs her*]

FIREMAN 3: Got her! Quick disarm her. [*FIREMAN 1 and FIREMAN 2 pile in blindly*] Get off! That's my neck!

FIREMAN 2: Sorry - I'll clean my windows. [*Wipes his gas mask*]

FIREMAN 1: Hang onto her.

FIREMAN 3: She's down here.

FIREMAN 1: We'll hold her still. Get the chloroform-mask.

WOMAN: Bastards! Get off!

FIREMAN 2: Which one is it?

FIREMAN 1: [*Pointing to YOUNG MAN*] Try it on him. [*To FIREMAN 3*] What kept you?

FIREMAN 3: Sorry Chief, faulty train taken out of service at Chalk Farm. No cash on me so I had to smash the barriers. The guard came after me.

WOMAN: Let go, scum!

FIREMAN 3: Shut up!

FIREMAN 1: [*To FIREMAN 3*] Put your hand over her mouth.

FIREMAN 2: I wouldn't put your hand anywhere near her mouth.

YOUNG MAN: [*Having been helped up*] You're... so... sexy...

FIREMAN 2: [*Holding mask on*] Thank you.

YOUNG MAN: Take me. [*He collapses*]

WOMAN: Prat!

FIREMAN 2: [*Removes mask*] It's this one. [*They place it on WOMAN, she collapses*]

FIREMAN 1: Come on. [*To FIREMAN 2*] You drugged him, you can carry him.

[*FIREMAN 2 picks up YOUNG MAN and carries him cradle fashion*]

[*Exeunt*]

FIREMAN 1: You've forgotten what we came for.

FIREMAN 3: [*Dashes back. Picks up WOMAN over his shoulder*] Every man for himself! [*He runs out commando style*]

[*Lights down*]

☐

INTERMEZZO

The intermezzo is a topical stand-up comedy routine between acts, and is updated on a day by day basis: Fo's *Intermezzo* - delivered by Franca Rame began like this.

Ladies and gentlemen, I'd like to take advantage of the scene change to clear up something rather important about the text of this play. To come to the point - what is this play of ours about? What is the message? The brighter ones among you will have cottoned on already. We have here a script in defence of the rich. Of course Dario Fo doesn't have much of a reputation in this field. On more than a few occasions he has admittedly weighed in with some pretty heavy satire against the wealthy and powerful. But surely he is entitled like everyone else to second thoughts...

☐

SCENE 2

Lights up on an ice-cream warehouse. There is a telephone, a fridge and a small table with a portable TV and a walkie-talkie. Stairs lead from the upper floor, at the foot of the stairs is a small piece of furniture on which there are a few bottles, a fire extinguisher, and a rope.

[*The WOMAN, trussed up blindfolded and gagged, is dragged in by two KIDNAPPERS dressed as firemen. They undo the ropes. She is very red and gesticulating frantically*]

CHIEF KIDNAPPER: What's wrong with her?

KIDNAPPER 2: Looks upset about something.

[*KIDNAPPER 3 enters on stairs he is holding a gas mask*]

CHIEF KIDNAPPER: You can take the tape off.

KIDNAPPER 2: I'd rather someone else...

KIDNAPPER 3: [*Rushing downstairs*] I'll do it. [*Rips off tape*]

WOMAN: [*Gasping*] I could hardly breath. Sadistic morons! I told you I've got a cold. You should be certified, locked up, *Strung up!*

KIDNAPPER 2: Told you she looked upset.

KIDNAPPER 3: I'll slap her around a bit.

CHIEF KIDNAPPER: No! She'll depreciate.

WOMAN: So! Pea-brains! You're expecting a ransom for me?

KIDNAPPER 2: Oh no, we collect media bosses. Rupert Murdoch's in the cellar.

WOMAN: I see! You think you've kidnapped Diana Forbes-McKaye, the media magnate?

KIDNAPPER 3: Yeah!

WOMAN: Owner of three newspapers, a cable network and most of a broadcast channel?

KIDNAPPER 2: Right!

WOMAN: Mother of two, who's recent marital separation and associated infidelities have been the media event of the decade?

CHIEF KIDNAPPER: That's the one!

WOMAN: Well you haven't! You have however kidnapped Josie Gordon, actor, impressionist, singer and comedienne but definitely not a businesswoman. And precisely which breed of insect are you?

KIDNAPPER 3: [*Adopting marshal-arts pose*] One swift kick to the head.

CHIEF KIDNAPPER: Calm down! [*To WOMAN*] What did you say?

WOMAN: An easy mistake to make, I am a remarkably convincing double. Though you'd think with this much at stake someone would've checked. Untie me, remove the blindfold and I'll forget all about the inconvenience.

CHIEF KIDNAPPER: [*To KIDNAPPER 3*] Is this true?

KIDNAPPER 3: It's a trick! I've been trailing her for months, got all the notes, photos, a video...

KIDNAPPER 2: If you're a comedienne, let's hear a bit of your routine.

WOMAN: Alright! Here goes then. A question for you. Why are women so bad at parking? Because they're always being told this [*Holding thumb and index finger a little way apart*] is eight inches. [*KIDNAPPER 2 has hysterics*]

KIDNAPPER 3: She's not a comedienne.

CHIEF KIDNAPPER: Let's take a closer look - masks on. [*KIDNAPPER 2 goes to put on gas mask*] No not that one. [*Goes to cupboard*] These party masks.
[*The three KIDNAPPERS go to put on caricature masks, the following are suggested character masks: CHIEF puts on John Major mask and KIDNAPPER 3 Saddam Hussein - KIDNAPPER 2 then goes picks out Margaret Thatcher mask*]

CHIEF KIDNAPPER: I'd rather you didn't use that one. [*Takes out Prince Charles mask*]
[*KIDNAPPER 2 puts it on; KIDNAPPER 3 then takes blindfold off the Woman*]

WOMAN: My god! *Spitting Image*!

KIDNAPPER 3: See it is her. Look at these photos. [*Hands them around*]

KIDNAPPER 2: This one's out of focus.

KIDNAPPER 3: It was a tricky shot. In this hotel, I had to stand on a reproduction Chesterfield, then the concierge's hat was in the way.

KIDNAPPER 2: What did you do?

KIDNAPPER 3: Surprised him with a dead-leg then a short-arm jab to the kidneys.

CHIEF KIDNAPPER: [*Looking at a different one*] Which one's her?

KIDNAPPER 3: That one. In the window, fourth from the right... Sixth floor.

[*They all three squint at the snapshot turn it around etc*]

KIDNAPPER 2: What setting did you use?

KIDNAPPER 3: Cloudy I think!

[*They look through the other photos*]

KIDNAPPER 2: Didn't you use the 80-240 zoom I gave you?

KIDNAPPER 3: Course I did. Only I was in Stringfellows and some jerk shut the toilet door on it. Now it's all bent.

KIDNAPPER 2: [*To CHIEF*] You should've left it to me, these are useless.

KIDNAPPER 3: [*To CHIEF*] We should never've of let him in on it, he always causes trouble.

CHIEF KIDNAPPER: Lads! Lads! Lets not argue amongst ourselves. [*To KIDNAPPER 3*] Is there any other way of identifying her?

WOMAN: D'you have a copy of *Spotlight*? The Actors Directory?

KIDNAPPER 3: That's it, the magazines in the cupboard. I've collected everyone she's been in, they'll prove it.

KIDNAPPER 2: [*Taking magazines out of cupboard*] *Vogue, the Economist, Creative Review, Spectator, Sunday Sport, War-Zone Gazette.*

KIDNAPPER 3: That's mine.

WOMAN: Infant!

KIDNAPPER 3: [*Madly pointing finger*] You're lucky I don't have a kalashnikov.

WOMAN: [*To CHIEF*] Is he stable?

KIDNAPPER 3: Shut it!

[*CHIEF holds pictures next to WOMAN's face*]

KIDNAPPER 2: It looks like her.

WOMAN: I'm supposed to, I'm a double! I'm appearing on the BBC for her tomorrow.

KIDNAPPER 2: Must be her. I don't know though... I'm not sure she looks quite evil enough.

CHIEF KIDNAPPER: Remember her in the apartment about to Black & Decker us into the wall.

KIDNAPPER 2: True!

CHIEF KIDNAPPER: [*Pulling the other two aside*] What do we reckon?

KIDNAPPER 3: Course it's her. She's taking us for a ride. Leave it to me. I'll prove it. [*CHIEF nods. KIDNAPPER 3 takes KID-*

NAPPER 2 aside] Play along with me we'll scare the truth out of her.

KIDNAPPER 2: Right! I get it!

KIDNAPPER 3: [To WOMAN] The Chief believes you; that you're not McKaye.

WOMAN: Good!

KIDNAPPER 3: So, Josie..."Comedienne": it's my job to deliver you.

WOMAN: Well you mustn't put yourself out, I'm sure I'll find my own way back.

KIDNAPPER 3: Oh no, I'll deliver you right to the steps of Broadcasting House.

WOMAN: If you insist.

KIDNAPPER 3: In a bin-liner.

KIDNAPPER 2: Yeah, in a bin-liner!

WOMAN: What?... No... Look... What for?

CHIEF KIDNAPPER: [To KIDNAPPER 3] OK! Kill her. But do it outside. I know you, you'll make a mess. [To KIDNAPPER 2] Get the bin-liner.

KIDNAPPER 2: [Whispering] No Chief, it's a ploy. [CHIEF pushes him toward the kitchen]

WOMAN: What good will it do?

KIDNAPPER 2: Yeah what good will it do? [Desperately whispering in his ear] It's only pretend. [KIDNAPPER 3 enters with a meat cleaver]

CHIEF KIDNAPPER: The bin-liner! [KIDNAPPER 2 exits to kitchen]

WOMAN: Mrs. McKaye won't care if I'm dead.

CHIEF KIDNAPPER: Nor will we - that's not the point.

[KIDNAPPER 3 starts business with the meat cleaver]

CHIEF KIDNAPPER: In this business it's the gesture that counts. It's not like fishing - catch a tiddler, throw it back, no one knows. We'd be a laughing stock.

[KIDNAPPER 2 returns with bin-liner]

CHIEF KIDNAPPER: OK, may as well take the masks off, she's not going to live to identify us.

[CHIEF reaches for his mask]

KIDNAPPER 2: [Still trying to stop him] No!

WOMAN: Stop! Keep them on. It's true. I am Diana Forbes-McKaye.

KIDNAPPER 3: Told you she'd break.

KIDNAPPER 2: [*To CHIEF*] You mean you knew? You were very convincing, I thought you were really going to...

CHIEF KIDNAPPER: Explain the situation to him would you.

KIDNAPPER 3: [*He hits KIDNAPPER 2*] Arsehole!

CHIEF KIDNAPPER: Eloquently put. [*To KIDNAPPER 2*] Go and check on Romeo.

    [*KIDNAPPER 2 exits*]

CHIEF KIDNAPPER: [*Going back to WOMAN*] Convince us.

WOMAN: I can tell you... The school I attended, my star-sign, the name of my husband's polo horse, a list of my investments, mother's maiden name... anything.

CHIEF KIDNAPPER: [*To KIDNAPPER 3*] Convinced?

KIDNAPPER 3: [*Playing with meat cleaver*] Nope!

WOMAN: Alright, alright then; I can tell you about a scandal...
    [*KIDNAPPER 3 immediately produces mini-cassette recorder as the CHIEF pulls out a notebook and pencil*]

WOMAN: Fraud... I'm under investigation, because there are allegations that inside information...

CHIEF KIDNAPPER: So tell me Mrs. Diana Forbes-McKaye, from where is it alleged that this inside information came?

WOMAN: The Home Office.

CHIEF KIDNAPPER: Ahha!
    [*Scribbles frantically in note book*]

KIDNAPPER 3: [*Holding his microphone closer*] A bit louder please darling.

WOMAN: The Home Office.

CHIEF KIDNAPPER: So it is alleged that you are involved in a major fraud in which the government of this country is complicit.?

WOMAN: That's right.

KIDNAPPER 3: A picture of her with the Home Secretary and the headline reads "Beauty and the Beast stitch up the small screen".

CHIEF KIDNAPPER: And how is it alleged that the inside information was obtained?
    [*KIDNAPPER 2 re-enters with YOUNG MAN*]

KIDNAPPER 3: Yeah, was a cabinet minister involved?
   [*CHIEF and KIDNAPPER 3 crowd around her*]
   Did you sleep with anyone?

CHIEF KIDNAPPER: How much money changed hands?

KIDNAPPER 3: Do you have any sexy photos?

CHIEF KIDNAPPER: Was the Prime Minister aware of the document?
   [*KIDNAPPER 2 seeing what is happening grabs a camera from the
   table and starts taking pictures wildly*]

WOMAN: Jesus! Who are you?

CHIEF KIDNAPPER: [*Putting notebook away*] Kidnappers!

KIDNAPPERS 2 & 3: [*Putting the camera/tape recorder down*] Kidnappers! Kidnappers!

KIDNAPPER 3: Told you it was her.

CHIEF KIDNAPPER: [*Getting into a conspiratorial huddle with the
   other kidnappers*] This is our insurance, anything goes wrong, we
   sell the story, as an exclusive. I'll write it up.

KIDNAPPER 2: I'll get some pics.

KIDNAPPER 3: I'll do a probing interview, I learnt some techniques
   from my mate in the West Midlands Serious Crime Squad.

WOMAN: What are you whispering about?

KIDNAPPERS 2 & 3: The weather! Politics! Sex!

CHIEF KIDNAPPER: [*Seeing YOUNG MAN*] Ah, a second opin-
   ion. [*Pointing at Woman*] Who is this?

YOUNG MAN: In what sense who is it?

CHIEF KIDNAPPER: Don't give me existentialism. Is it McKaye
   or a double?

YOUNG MAN: I'm not sure, I think it's McKaye...

WOMAN: There we are. What did I tell you?

YOUNG MAN: Before we... er before she er... earlier on; she had a
   ruby, that big, on her finger, but when you lot...

WOMAN: Thank you Kevin. You've answered the question.

YOUNG MAN: When you burst, in the first thing she did was take
   it off and hide it.

WOMAN: Traitor! You're easily bought.

YOUNG MAN: If it was false she wouldn't have bothered.

CHIEF KIDNAPPER: What was the ring like?

YOUNG MAN: A high carat Ruby. Fine clean stone too. Emerald cut, rub over...

CHIEF KIDNAPPER: How come you know so much about it?

YOUNG MAN: Did an ET programme with Ratners - never saw anything like that. Must be worth a few thousand, no actor could afford that.

KIDNAPPER 2: A bit like Poirot isn't he.

WOMAN: The important thing is that he's confirmed who I am. Let us turn our attention to this ransom situation. The ring, as it happens, was paste though it had sentimental value. Unfortunately with all the goings-on, I lost it...

YOUNG MAN: It's down her front.

WOMAN: Judas! [*To others*] It slipped down, don't know where it...

CHIEF KIDNAPPER: You'll have to undress!

YOUNG MAN: Oh good!

WOMAN: Quiet turncoat!

KIDNAPPER 2: [*Going to fetch it*] The camera!

CHIEF KIDNAPPER: [*Thinking aloud*] "Television Tycoon is Teasing Temptress".

KIDNAPPER 2: "Di Bares her Assets".

KIDNAPPER 3: "Di's-gusting".

WOMAN: Never will I so cheapen myself that I'd...

CHIEF KIDNAPPER: She needs a hand!

KIDNAPPER 3: [*Approaching with meat cleaver*] I'll help!

WOMAN: Aaah! No! I've changed my mind... I'll find it. [*Wriggles*] It seems to be down my tights. Turn your heads.

CHIEF KIDNAPPER: No, we reserve rights to the whole show.
[*CHIEF and KIDNAPPER 3 pop party poppers throw streamers etc. at her whilst KIDNAPPER 2 gets the pictures*]

KIDNAPPER 2: [*With the camera*] Turn towards me love.

WOMAN: Animals!

KIDNAPPER 2: We need an ogler, someone seedy, depraved.

KIDNAPPER 3: You're depraved. [*CHIEF and KIDNAPPER 3 manoeuvre YOUNG MAN into appropriate voyeuristic pose*]

KIDNAPPER 2: [*To YOUNG MAN*] Open your mouth. Wider. Drool a bit... Eyes on stalks. Lovely!

KIDNAPPER 3: Wave this at her.

[*Hands YOUNG MAN ten pound note*]

YOUNG MAN: I was in this club once and...

ALL: Shut up turncoat!

WOMAN: It's slipped down to my knee... I can't get it up. [*Lots of giggling and laughter*] You'll have to loosen my ankles.

CHIEF KIDNAPPER: Carry on as you are.

KIDNAPPER 2: More sex darling! Ooze for the camera!

CHIEF KIDNAPPER: [*To YOUNG MAN*] Help her out. [*To others*] He's already had some hands-on experience.

[*More laughter*]

WOMAN: Don't touch me, turncoat.

YOUNG MAN: [*Whispering to WOMAN*] Don't get worked up I'm saving your life. [*She has worked ring up to top of tights. He picks it out*] Here it is!

KIDNAPPER 3: [*Darts toward them with meat cleaver*] Let's see. [*They scream*] Well done turncoat.

CHIEF KIDNAPPER: Give it here; not bad. [*Takes ring over to cabinet*] We'll count this with our earnings.

WOMAN: Common thieves as well as incompetent kidnappers.

[*KIDNAPPER 3 moves toward her menacingly*]

CHIEF KIDNAPPER: [*To KIDNAPPER 3*] For Christ's sake put that thing back in the kitchen.

[*KIDNAPPER 3 exits*]

KIDNAPPER 2: [*To YOUNG MAN*] Hey, did you two... Actually, did you, well... you know... did she... What exactly did you two get up to in the apartment before we arrived?

YOUNG MAN: First she blindfolded me...

WOMAN: *Kevin!*

YOUNG MAN: Er... She said I have very soft skin.

KIDNAPPER 2: [*Touching his cheek*] Oh yes, it is quite soft.

KIDNAPPER 3: [*Bursting in through kitchen door*] Chief!

CHIEF KIDNAPPER: What is it?

KIDNAPPER 3: Hot off the presses. [*Produces papers*] We're in 'em. [*The other two gather round*] Not the coverage we'd hoped for...

WOMAN: What does it say?

CHIEF KIDNAPPER: This is private business, sit down. [*To KIDNAPPER 3*] Try and keep your voice down.

KIDNAPPER 3: [*All three now adopt hushed conspiratorial tones*] The headline is "Police bungle arrest of media Baroness".

KIDNAPPER 2: They could've had "Met don't stick to magnate".

KIDNAPPER 3: It says "Police arrived just two minutes after Diana Forbes-McKaye was seen leaving in a Ford Transit".

CHIEF KIDNAPPER: Two minutes! That was quick!

KIDNAPPER 2: Or "Di foils DI".

KIDNAPPER 3: They were tipped off!

KIDNAPPER 2: Who?

CHIEF KIDNAPPER: The police?

KIDNAPPER 3: The Police arrived with Willoughby.

WOMAN: [*In same hushed tones*] My PR man!

CHIEF KIDNAPPER: Shhh!

KIDNAPPER 3: [*Reading*] "Willoughby is Mrs. McKaye's PR man".

YOUNG MAN: Doesn't mention me does it?

WOMAN: Why should it mention you?

CHIEF KIDNAPPER: Will you two keep out of this. [*Hushed tones again*] How did they know?

KIDNAPPER 2: Who?

CHIEF KIDNAPPER: The police.

KIDNAPPER 3: Know what?

CHIEF KIDNAPPER: About the kidnapping.

KIDNAPPER 3: They hadn't come for the kidnapping.

KIDNAPPER 2: Who hadn't?

KIDNAPPER 3: The police.

CHIEF KIDNAPPER: What!

KIDNAPPER 3: They were coming to arrest her.

KIDNAPPER 2: Who? [*KIDNAPPER 3 hits him*]

WOMAN: [*Laughing*] Wonderful; the Serious Fraud squad.

KIDNAPPER 3: [*Reading*] "Following the allegations, police are uncertain whether the kidnapping is a put-up job".

CHIEF KIDNAPPER: I don't believe it!

KIDNAPPER 2: I know! What a cumbersome sentence.

KIDNAPPER 3: It's all there. [*Passes the newspaper*]

CHIEF KIDNAPPER: [*Reading*] "The Police had earlier mistakenly arrested the Diana double, Josie Gordon... The matter was later cleared up and the double released".

KIDNAPPER 3: [*Looking through other papers*] All about the fraud case, nothing about the kidnapping. Apart from this one... [*Holds up tabloid with full page picture of Diana*]

WOMAN: Ahh! That's one of mine.

KIDNAPPER 3: ...a three-paged article headed "Don't let her Di".

CHIEF KIDNAPPER: [*Tearing pages out of his notebook*] So much for our exclusive.

KIDNAPPER 2: We still got the photos. And we got her.

WOMAN: Thank you so much; it appears you rescued me in the nick of time from a very awkward little scene. We ought to celebrate! Let's have a couple of bottles of champagne, on my account.

YOUNG MAN: Great! I'll go! [*Prepares to go*]

WOMAN: Pass the phone, I need to arrange a few leaked stories. [*KIDNAPPER 2 picks up the phone*]

CHIEF KIDNAPPER: [*To KIDNAPPER 2*] Put it down! [*To YOUNG MAN*] Stay where you are! We're not celebrating anything.

KIDNAPPER 3: Yeah, two minutes later and we'd be in a cell now... or shot.

YOUNG MAN: [*Setting off*] I know this really nice little off licence...

CHIEF KIDNAPPER: [*Stopping him*] Sit down! Everybody! I need some quiet so I can evaluate the implications of this new situation.

KIDNAPPER 3: Evaluate! Cut a couple of her fingers off and send them to ITN, then they'll take the kidnapping seriously.

CHIEF KIDNAPPER: Shut up! Testosterone crazed lunatic! We are not supposed to damage her.

KIDNAPPER 3: [*Grabbing him*] Least I got testosterones! [*KIDNAPPER 2 separates them*]

WOMAN: Don't squabble! We've hit a little hurdle, I...

CHIEF KIDNAPPER: A little hurdle! They think we're working for you.

KIDNAPPER 3: Cut her ear off! Then they'll...

WOMAN: A sense of proportion, please!

CHIEF KIDNAPPER: Not another word, or he starts work on your extremities.

KIDNAPPER 2: An idea! We take her round different places, photograph her near landmarks. Then sell the photos, she'd be like Lord Lucan, the media'd love it.

CHIEF KIDNAPPER: This is a carefully planned kidnapping...
[*WOMAN laughs*]... we've done as instructed now we sit tight and
wait for news. If we turn this into a "Spot the Diana" competition
we will end up in prison as accomplices to her fraud.

KIDNAPPER 2: What a bummer! [*Holding up a newspaper*] We spend
weeks planning a hideous crime and she ends up getting the credit.

WOMAN: [*Reading the paper*] At least my little tabloids are taking it
seriously. Aaah! They've started a fund for my ransom money.

KIDNAPPER 2: [*Having a look*] Now that's well thought out. If you
send in a fiver you get an extra bingo card, a badge saying "I dug
deep for Di" and 10% off all items at Halfords.

WOMAN: A number of readers have already dug into their savings and
they are trying to locate my estranged husband for a contribution.

CHIEF KIDNAPPER: Well that's encouraging.

KIDNAPPER 2: Heart warming.

WOMAN: I shouldn't get excited. My husband is deranged. He's
probably saving a whale or a panda or a rain-forest. He's into
causes, unfortunately for you I'm not one of them.

CHIEF KIDNAPPER: I'm beginning to feel quite depressed about
the whole situation.

WOMAN: I, on the other hand, have a quite brilliant plan.

YOUNG MAN: Good, lets celebrate. Champagne anyone?

WOMAN: You'll get a tidy sum and I'll be free to exploit the situation
for all its worth.

YOUNG MAN: Let's drink to that. I'll pop down to the off licence.

CHIEF KIDNAPPER: No one is drinking champagne!

WOMAN: Obviously, you have a boss, an insider who set the whole
thing up. Someone who works in TV...? Who knows me...?

KIDNAPPER 2: That's right he...

CHIEF KIDNAPPER: Not another word!

WOMAN: I see! Trying to salvage a little professional pride? Lets
face facts, the person you are relying upon to pay the ransom will
be running in to severe difficulties. The only money available is
in my personal account. So we need to work together.

CHIEF KIDNAPPER: Why are you so keen to get arrested?

WOMAN: Kidnapping isn't the only thing you know nothing about.
Let me explain. We live in a democracy which means power lies
in the hands of...?

CHIEF KIDNAPPER: The government?

WOMAN: No!

KIDNAPPER 3: The police!

WOMAN: No!

KIDNAPPER 2: The people.

CHIEF & KIDNAPPER 3: No!

WOMAN: Power rests with those able to inform and influence the nodding majority. In short, me! So for the fraud charges against me it's a case of assisting the public to look at it in a different light...

KIDNAPPER 2: Brainwashing?

WOMAN: Oh no! Re-directing, re-educating, so the public see this not as a city fraud case but as a government scandal.

CHIEF KIDNAPPER: How convenient!

WOMAN: Precisely! In a new twist, a journalist will have discovered that I had been having an affair with junior Home Office minister.

KIDNAPPER 3: "Di screws Home Office".

KIDNAPPER 2: "McKaye's Man from the Ministry".

KIDNAPPER 3: [*Holding his tape recorder*] What's his name? How long you been doing it together? Ever do it in a Chelsea kit?

WOMAN: Infinitely more interesting than a complicated business fraud. A witch hunt has begun. Which ministers knew about it? Which ones are implicated? Which information was available to the Prime Minister? The government can do what it likes to the economy; but a sex scandal, that really gets the punters going.

KIDNAPPER 3: What about the Old Bill?

WOMAN: Charges will be dropped in an attempt to minimise damage to the government. They will, of course, institute a parliamentary enquiry which will be a tiny bit critical of "The timing of certain discussions". The afore-mentioned junior minister will resign and the whole matter will then be forgotten.

[*KIDNAPPER 2 and KIDNAPPER 3 both clap wildly*]

KIDNAPPER 2: Brilliant!

CHIEF KIDNAPPER: I'm in charge here!

[*KIDNAPPER 3 is standing behind him making bunny ears*]

CHIEF KIDNAPPER: [*To WOMAN*] I'll gag you again.

WOMAN: Go ahead! Lose the chance of sharing a million pounds.

KIDNAPPER 3: Bloody hell!

KIDNAPPER 2: That's more than we were offered.

YOUNG MAN: A million!

WOMAN: [*To YOUNG MAN*] Not you, traitor.

   [*The walkie-talkie starts bleeping*]

KIDNAPPER 3: What's that!

CHIEF KIDNAPPER: The walkie-talkie.

KIDNAPPER 2: What shall we do?

CHIEF KIDNAPPER: Answer it.

KIDNAPPER 3: Hullo... er, sorry... receiving... yes, "Raspberry Ripple" here... go ahead Pistachio... yes all in order... What shall we do with the "parcel"... Why? Oh, hang on. I'll hand you over to Tutti Frutti. [*Offers it to CHIEF*]

CHIEF KIDNAPPER: [*Pointing to KIDNAPPER 2*] No, he's Tutti Frutti, I'm Rum & Raisin.

[*KIDNAPPER 3 hands it over*]

CHIEF KIDNAPPER: Rum & Raisin here, what's the low- down? Well it means, what's going on, you know - what's happening... Oh haven't you, well it's quite a well known phrase. Right... OK... What d'you mean "damp"?

WOMAN: I think you'll find he means - fuck-up.

CHIEF KIDNAPPER: [*Hand over mouth-piece*] Try to keep her quiet.

KIDNAPPER 3: [*To WOMAN*] Shut up or I'll kill you!

CHIEF KIDNAPPER: Right... Well don't get "soaked" yourself... Yes, OK... Cheers.

   [*Puts the walkie-talkie back*] He hasn't arranged a rendezvous.

WOMAN: What a surprise!

CHIEF KIDNAPPER: Unforeseen problems.

WOMAN: Dear oh dear!

CHIEF KIDNAPPER: There are stories leaking and bursting out all over the place, it's a reporters Shangri-La.

WOMAN: It grieves me to say it but... I told you so.

KIDNAPPER 3: Why don't you let me kill her?

CHIEF KIDNAPPER: I'm beginning to wonder.

KIDNAPPER 2: Shangri-La! Aren't they a sixties pop group?

KIDNAPPER 3: [*Switching it on*] Let's see the TV news.

CHIEF KIDNAPPER: Alright, but BBC. We're not watching her channel.

TV: The BBC has acquired this exclusive amateur video, showing the unfortunate Diana McKaye being ruthlessly abducted and bundled into a Ford Transit by three desperate criminals.

KIDNAPPER 2: That's a good shot of you Chief!

CHIEF KIDNAPPER: Who the bloody hell was shooting a home movie in a residential street in Golders Green?

TV: Across the nation people have been shocked by the kidnapping of the much loved media boss. Trustees of the "Dig Deep for Diana" fund are offering a family holiday at Disney World and £1000 spending money for information leading to Diana's release. So if you have any information just go to any branch of Thomas Cooke or contact the police on 0898 987654 - calls will be charged at 38p per minute.

[*YOUNG MAN is surreptitiously writing down the number*]

KIDNAPPER 2: [*Seeing him*] Oi! give that here.

[*KIDNAPPER 2 tries to take the slip of paper off him and chases YOUNG MAN who runs into KIDNAPPER 3 and immediately gives up the paper*]

CHIEF KIDNAPPER: [*To KIDNAPPER 3*] Destroy it!

[*KIDNAPPER 3 eats the paper*]

CHIEF KIDNAPPER: Turn the TV off it's making me sick.

WOMAN: Are you ready to hear my plan?

KIDNAPPER 2: It can't make things any worse.

WOMAN: This is what we do. Remove the unnecessary layer of business activity...

KIDNAPPER 3: Yeah!

WOMAN: Cut out the middle-man...

KIDNAPPER 3: Yeah!

WOMAN ...who stands to cream off a huge commission for doing sod-all. Or, in layman's terms, "the estate agent syndrome".

YOUNG MAN: My uncle's an estate agent.

WOMAN: Free consultancy on how to be better criminals: you've got to think big. Get the maximum return on your investment. Now! What have you invested?

KIDNAPPER 2: [*They look at each other*] Er... that's a tough one...

WOMAN: Your liberty... you have risked your freedom... invested it, in this project. If it fails you stand to loose your investment.

KIDNAPPER 3: Be banged up or shot!

WOMAN: Well done! [*KIDNAPPER 3 looks pleased with himself*] Now you are expecting a return on this investment in the form of...? [*No response*] ...Ransom money. [*Sighs of frustration at missing out on the answer*] At the moment, you don't stand to gain very much. See what I'm getting at?

KIDNAPPERS 2 & 3: No!

WOMAN: Your investment is represented by your captive - in this instance me. [*Pointing to YOUNG MAN*] You can be the captive - you've the look of a natural victim.

YOUNG MAN: You mean I've got to be - you?

WOMAN: [*To KIDNAPPER 3*] And if you could represent his captors.

KIDNAPPER 3: Right OK.

WOMAN: Perhaps you should tie him up, give it a little authenticity.

KIDNAPPER 3: [*Frantically tying him up*] Good idea!

YOUNG MAN: Ouch that's too tight. That hurts.

KIDNAPPER 2: Shut up Kevin. This is role play.

YOUNG MAN: My name is not Kevin.

WOMAN: [*To KIDNAPPER 2*] You are the leader of the captors the link with the boss... or middle-man.

KIDNAPPER 2: I see! So I'm sort of like... the Chief, here? [*He starts some elaborate pacing and general anxious acting*] [*In obviously posher accent*] I and my brave men [*Slapping KIDNAPPER 3 heartily on the back*] have successfully captured the establishment's propaganda peddler and now we must wait. Oh the worry, as Chief the weight of responsibility rests...

WOMAN: Thank you! We don't need a soliloquy. [*To CHIEF*] If you...

KIDNAPPER 2: What sort of social background do I have? I think there's a bit of ambiguity...

CHIEF KIDNAPPER: What are you suggesting...?

WOMAN: [*To KIDNAPPER 2*] Just stand there; next to the other captor. [*To CHIEF*] Now you come over here and sit by the phone. You are going to be our man on the inside. The boss or middle-man. [*All boo and hiss*] Let us begin. We'll assume that by some miracle everything goes according to plan. Our captive is released.

YOUNG MAN: Hurray!

WOMAN: The money is handed over to the Boss. [*Boos etc.*] You've never seen the Boss...

KIDNAPPER 2: That's right we haven't...

CHIEF KIDNAPPER: Shut up!

WOMAN: You get the news through the walkie-talkie. [*KIDNAPPER 2 picks up walkie-talkie*] The exchange has taken place and you will receive your share of the ransom via a messenger.

KIDNAPPER 2: [*In his "CHIEF" voice*] Yes... OK. Thank you very much sir... Cheers. [*To KIDNAPPER 3*] He says the exchange has taken place and we will receive our share of the ransom via a messenger.

WOMAN: Good!

KIDNAPPER 2: Thank you... You don't think the delivery was a bit quick?

CHIEF KIDNAPPER: Look, Dustin, can we get on with this.

WOMAN: To keep it simple we'll say the ransom was £100. [*To CHIEF KIDNAPPER*] Take your percentage and the messenger takes the rest.
[*CHIEF KIDNAPPER gets £25 out wallet. WOMAN takes it to KIDNAPPER 2*]

KIDNAPPER 2: Thank you very much messenger. [*Melodramatic gesture*] Twenty-five quid, is that all. Here's you half. [*Hands KIDNAPPER 3 £10*]

KIDNAPPER 3: Ten quid! [*To CHIEF*] Bastard! I've risked my life for a tenner. What happened to all the rest of the money? [*Goes over to CHIEF*] I'm going to 'ave you!

KIDNAPPER 2: [*To WOMAN*] He can't do that! He's walked through the wall. [*To KIDNAPPER 3*] You've walked through the wall! We don't know him, you see...

KIDNAPPER 3: Shut up! I know him alright he's trying to rip us off. [*They square up to each other*]

CHIEF KIDNAPPER: If it wasn't for my contacts in the City you wouldn't have been able to do the thing at all, and there's my expenses... renting the hideaway, the Transit Van etc. £100 doesn't go far.

KIDNAPPER 3: Thieving City bastard! [*Fight starts- WOMAN comes between them*]

WOMAN: Alright! That's it! The first scenario. Now lets see what will happen to you, if it all goes wrong. Positions please! [*Claps her hands*]

YOUNG MAN: What about me?

WOMAN: Well, it's all gone wrong, so, you're finished. [*To KIDNAPPER 3*] Would you?

[*KIDNAPPER 3 walks up to YOUNG MAN punches him in the face - YOUNG MAN collapses on the floor, he is out cold*]

WOMAN: Thank you! And the rest of you are in court. We are a little short of numbers so I'll have to be the Judge and Jury...

CHIEF KIDNAPPER: That's not fair!

WOMAN: [*Using walkie-talkie as gavel*] Silence! Or I'll have you charged with contempt.

KIDNAPPER 2: [*Whispering*] She's very good!

KIDNAPPER 3: Very life-like.

WOMAN: To sum up! [*She comes out from behind the table, starts pacing*] Let's consider the defendants, one by one. First, this man. [*Points walkie-talkie at KIDNAPPER 3*] There were the witnesses who identified him as having followed the deceased, with the camera with the wonky lens. It has been proved beyond all doubt that he abducted and illegally incarcerated the deceased and also that he was a party to the demanding of a ransom for the deceased.

KIDNAPPER 2: She knows all the terms.

WOMAN: Finally, his finger prints all over the murder weapon suggest, that it was his hands that committed the murder.

KIDNAPPER 3: Why did I let them take me alive!

WOMAN: [*Pointing walkie-talkie at KIDNAPPER 2*] To this man. He forced his way into the deceased's apartment disguised as a fireman. And once again that he, with his colleague, did abduct and incarcerate the deceased is proved beyond doubt. He was in a position of some influence over his colleague and is therefore an accomplice to...

KIDNAPPER 2: No, it was him! it's not my fault! He's a psychopath!

KIDNAPPER 3: [*Lunging at KIDNAPPER 2*] Call me a psychopath and live?

WOMAN: [*Frantically banging the walkie-talkie*] I will have order in my court. To the third defendant. [*Points walkie-talkie at CHIEF*] What real evidence do we have against this gentleman? None! We know of his reputation as a pillar of the community, his many works for charity and we heard how he "cried buckets" on hearing the fate of the deceased. He is also a member of the Athenaeum, a club of which I myself am a member and I happen to know that he can finish *The Times* crossword in under twenty minutes. How's the wife?

CHIEF KIDNAPPER: We're hoping the trip down the Nile will do wonders for the gangrene.

WOMAN: To these testimonies against him. They claim that they saw his picture in a magazine and knew that "he was the geezer with the whiny voice that we talked to on the phone". When asked how they could identify him, they said "he had that non-descript, grey, blend-into-the-background look and anyway his eyes are too close together". Can we really condemn a man because his eyes happen to be close together? Or because he wears grey suits or has a whiny voice? I think not!

CHIEF KIDNAPPER: Well summed up, m'lord.

WOMAN: Thank you, old socks! So, to the verdicts. [*Pointing to KIDNAPPER 3 from behind table*] The first defendant, the charges are conspiracy to defraud, abduction and kidnapping, and murder. [*Darts out from behind table to be jury*] Guilty! [*Going back*] The further charge of fare evasion and damaging the property of London Underground. [*Getting carried away*] Guilty! I sentence you to life imprisonment and recommend you receive psychiatric care.

KIDNAPPER 3: You'll never break me!

WOMAN: The second defendant. The charges of conspiracy, abduction and murder. [*As before*] Guilty! And the further charge of theft of my... er the ruby ring. Guilty! I sentence you to life imprisonment.

KIDNAPPER 2: No you can't, please show mercy not for my sake but for my children...

KIDNAPPER 3: Coward! Take it like a man! You haven't got any children.

KIDNAPPER 2: Please Your Honour...

WOMAN: Silence, ring thief! To the third defendant. The charge is conspiring to kidnap and demand a ransom. Not Guilty!

CHIEF KIDNAPPER: Thank you, Your Honour.

WOMAN: [*To CHIEF*] Mine's a gin and tonic.

KIDNAPPER 3: What, you mean he can walk?

WOMAN: No evidence you see.

KIDNAPPER 3: He arranged the whole deal.

CHIEF KIDNAPPER: Sorry, do I know you?

WOMAN: No proof.

KIDNAPPER 3: [*To CHIEF*] If I'm going down you're coming with me. [*Picks up chair*]

CHIEF KIDNAPPER: Psychotic lout!

WOMAN: [*Coming between them*] Alright, stop! Settle down! The important thing is that you see that you're being ripped off!

KIDNAPPER 2: What do we do about it?

KIDNAPPER 3: A million you said.

WOMAN: We might be able to generate even more - when the fuss has died down a bit - we could sell your stories, my memoirs...

KIDNAPPER 2: Yeah!

WOMAN: A book, a television drama maybe...

KIDNAPPER 3: Yeah!

CHIEF KIDNAPPER: Kidnappers!

KIDNAPPER 3: Kidnappers!

YOUNG MAN: [*Waking up*] Aaah, I think my jaw's broken.

CHIEF KIDNAPPER: I'm in charge!

KIDNAPPER 2: Got to admit Chief, illegal deals are her area of expertise.

KIDNAPPER 3: [*To CHIEF*] Alright! So tell us, what do we do?

CHIEF KIDNAPPER: [*Holding the now wrecked walkie-talkie*] Don't have much choice now; making other arrangements will prove difficult. Go on. Let's hear your plan.

YOUNG MAN: If we've not heard anything Chief, I'm moving on, no ones looking for me...

WOMAN: What's all this *we*?

KIDNAPPER 2 and KIDNAPPER 3: Slip of the tongue! He meant *me*! He's delirious! etc.

WOMAN: You really are one of them, aren't you?

YOUNG MAN: Not exactly...

WOMAN: Treacherous bastard!

CHIEF KIDNAPPER: May as well come clean, Kevin.

KIDNAPPER 3: He was the bait.

WOMAN: Worm!

YOUNG MAN: It wasn't my idea...

WOMAN: You mean all that "you're so sexy, what an exciting woman, yes Mrs. McKaye, no Mrs. McKaye" was all acting.

YOUNG MAN: No honestly...

WOMAN: The bait! You... you... maggot!

KIDNAPPER 2: "Diana's worm turns".

YOUNG MAN: [*On his knees*] I had to.

CHIEF KIDNAPPER: Get up!

WOMAN: When all this is over, Kevin, you better get yourself a lot further away than Romford; because I'm going to come looking for you, and when I find you, I'm going to disembowel you!

YOUNG MAN: [*On his knees again*] No please...

[*KIDNAPPER 2 is taking photos*]

KIDNAPPER 3: "'E's for the chop".

KIDNAPPER 2: "McKaye menaces minor".

CHIEF KIDNAPPER: Kidnappers!

KIDNAPPERS 2 & 3: [*Putting away the camera*] Kidnappers! Kidnappers!

YOUNG MAN: Don't you think we should tie her hands?

CHIEF KIDNAPPER: Scared she might hop after you?

WOMAN: Keep him away from me.

CHIEF KIDNAPPER: Get up Kevin.

WOMAN: Don't mention his name!

YOUNG MAN: Can I go now?

CHIEF KIDNAPPER: No! There's been a change of plan.

YOUNG MAN: What's the new plan then?

KIDNAPPER 2: She's just about to tell us.

WOMAN: Gather round. [*All do so except YOUNG MAN*] Now we're going to cut out the middle man, yes?

KIDNAPPERS 2 & 3: Yeah!

WOMAN: OK! Given that your grasp of the principles of the market economy is so feeble; I think I better make the arrangements myself. Does that telephone still work?

CHIEF KIDNAPPER: Should do, you haven't touched that. Who are you going to phone?

WOMAN: My PR man...

KIDNAPPER 3: Aaah Willoughby, [*Going to get magazine from cupboard*] there's a picture of them together I found it in *Working Woman.* There look.

KIDNAPPER 2: Quite young, isn't he?

CHIEF KIDNAPPER: She's a bit of a cradle snatcher.

WOMAN: Voyeurs!

KIDNAPPER 3: Looks a bit like Kev... er... Maggot.

KIDNAPPER 2: Yeah! Stronger chin though and the suit...

KIDNAPPER 3: I like double-breasted.

KIDNAPPER 2: Yeah! Now that's Italian, linen double-breasted in camel, it is a lovely suit.

CHIEF KIDNAPPER: Too flashy for me, linen suits, especially the camel.

KIDNAPPER 2: Oh no, I think the camel is quite distinguished.

WOMAN: For Christ's sake! Are you kidnappers or fashion consultants?

KIDNAPPERS 2 & 3: Kidnappers! Kidnappers!

WOMAN: Hand me the phone. [*KIDNAPPER 2 goes to phone*]

CHIEF KIDNAPPER: Leave it there! Your beloved Willoughby's phone is bound to be tapped. You make the call and we're caught. It's a good job...

WOMAN: I'd already thought of that. Right now he'll be having lunch in the Gay Hussar in Soho, I'll phone him there.

KIDNAPPER 2: Nice try Chief.

WOMAN: I'll tell him to prepare himself for a big withdrawal.

KIDNAPPER 2: [*Sniggers. They all look at him*] Sorry.

WOMAN: Then I just fill in a cheque. Snoo... Willoughby will withdraw it and one of you, I suggest the Maggot as no one's looking for him, goes with him and picks it up.

YOUNG MAN: Yeah! I'll go!

CHIEF KIDNAPPER: Hold on! I'm a little confused.

WOMAN: I thought you might be.

CHIEF KIDNAPPER: Why are you so willing to part with all that money?

WOMAN: Much as I enjoy your company, I am being held captive. Secondly, whilst I trust my friends I would like to be clearing my name. Finally, publicity is my life blood, I have considerable clout because I can give a high profile to any project. So given the air time you've already generated, a million pounds is a bargain.

CHIEF KIDNAPPER: Alright, but we do it my way.

WOMAN: Of course! The telephone number and cheque-books are in my handbag. [*Points to it and KIDNAPPER 2 gets it*]

CHIEF KIDNAPPER: [*To KIDNAPPER 2*] Check it first.

KIDNAPPER 2: Right! [*Looks in bag*] Er... what am I looking for?

CHIEF KIDNAPPER: A weapon.

KIDNAPPER 2: Oh... [*Hands it to woman*] No weapons!

WOMAN: Thank you. [*Hands card to CHIEF*] The number.

CHIEF KIDNAPPER: I'm going to dial.

WOMAN: Oh good!

CHIEF KIDNAPPER: [*Dialling number*] No tricks, alright. Ah Hullo is that the Gay Hussar... [*Long pause*] ...I'm terribly sorry madam... wrong number. [*Re-dials*] [*To KIDNAPPER 3*] Get ready to hurt her if she tries anything! [*KIDNAPPER 3 runs off into the kitchen*] Oh hullo... Is that the Gay Hussar restaurant? I need to talk urgently with Mr. Willoughby, is he there? [*Handing her the receiver*] They're putting him on... no tricks.

WOMAN: Hi snookums, it's Diana... Keep calm and act naturally. I'm still with those... friends. Don't interrupt! Listen carefully! Be at... [*Covering mouthpiece*] Where? [*CHIEF makes gestures to show Tower Bridge*] Dartford Tunnel toll booths in an hour. Well, you'll have to drive fast won't you. Don't say anything to anyone and be alone or... [*KIDNAPPER 3 has returned with meat cleaver and is chopping up her pencil*] ...they'll take it out on me. A young man will come over to you. [*The CHIEF is frantically pointing to the Thatcher mask*] Oh, he'll have a face like Margaret Thatcher... No, no don't panic, it's only a mask... Yes, it'll be like dropping off the annual contribution to Central Office funds. Now shut up and listen! She... er he'll give you a signed cheque and your

instructions. Follow them to the letter! No cock ups! Oh and I
enjoyed the news coverage, well done. [*Blows him a kiss*] Bye bye
baby snookums. [*Puts phone down*] [*To Chief*] All done!
[*She starts writing in note book and filling in cheque*]

KIDNAPPER 2: Is Baby snookums a media term?

CHIEF KIDNAPPER: Let's get organised. [*To YOUNG MAN*] I'm
coming with you...

WOMAN: You're not leaving me with him, are you? [*Pointing at
KIDNAPPER 3*]

CHIEF KIDNAPPER: You're right! [*To KIDNAPPER 3*] You better
come too in case we run in to any trouble.

KIDNAPPER 2: You're not leaving me alone with...

KIDNAPPER 3: Shall I bring the meat cleaver?

CHIEF KIDNAPPER: Good idea.

KIDNAPPER 2: Chief! I have a problem with the...

CHIEF KIDNAPPER: [*To WOMAN*] Have you finished yet?

KIDNAPPER 2: Chief! Can I have a word, I'm not at all happy...

WOMAN: There! [*Handing cheque and note to CHIEF*] You'll get the
money in an attaché case that will be handcuffed to your wrist.

CHIEF KIDNAPPER: Who's got the key?

WOMAN: No key, the attaché case has a code number, which only I
know.

KIDNAPPER 2: Chief, I don't think it's safe leaving her with just me.

CHIEF KIDNAPPER: Why? What are you going to do?

KIDNAPPER 2: No I mean me, she might give me some trouble.
[*KIDNAPPER 3 laughs, points at KIDNAPPER 2 and starts
skipping on the spot in an exaggeratedly affected way*]

CHIEF KIDNAPPER: [*To KIDNAPPER 3*] Tie her up properly!
[*To KIDNAPPER 2*] Keep her gagged and blindfolded. You saw
Silence of the Lambs, she's Hannibal Lecter.

WOMAN: If you're going to gag me again can I clear my nose first.
There's some Vicks in my bag.

CHIEF KIDNAPPER: Come on, let's go. [*To KIDNAPPER 2*] You
OK?

KIDNAPPER 2: A bit nervous. [*Starts looking through her bag*]

CHIEF KIDNAPPER: Don't let her out of your sight or talk you in
to doing anything stupid. Watch out if she starts flattering you.
The walkie-talkie's bust so I'll use the phone. Cheers!

KIDNAPPER 3: See ya Rambo!

KIDNAPPER 2: Good luck.

WOMAN: A bientôt.

KIDNAPPER 2: What'd she say?

CHIEF KIDNAPPER: Hurry up and gag her. Keep your wits about you. [*They exit*]

WOMAN: Oik! Now have you found the Vicks?

KIDNAPPER 2: [*Takes out medical kit and syringe*] Are you an addict?

WOMAN: No, but I do have a weakness...

KIDNAPPER 2: [*Taking out a photo*] The Prime Minister [*Reading*] "Thanks for all your hard work, we owe it all to you". Signed J.M. - April '92.

WOMAN: That's personal. You're looking for the Vicks.

KIDNAPPER 2: Here it is! [*Offering it to her*]

WOMAN: You'll have to help me.

KIDNAPPER 2: I've never used one.

WOMAN: Don't worry! I'll talk you through. Unscrew the cap. How did you get involved with those crooks, you seem much more caring... Shake the bottle up. Interested in the finer things. Perhaps they're corrupting...?

KIDNAPPER 2: [*Covering his ears*] I'm not listening! It won't work! I've seen *Silence of the Lambs*. What do I do with this?

WOMAN: Insert the narrow end and squeeze the fat end.

KIDNAPPER 2: [*Holding bottle to tip of nose*] Like that?

WOMAN: Don't be shy, put it in. Come on. I'll do it myself, untie my hands.

KIDNAPPER 2: I'm not untying anything! [*Trying again*] How's that?

WOMAN: Great! Alright, don't push, you don't have to get the whole bottle up there. Now the other one.

KIDNAPPER 2: The other one.

WOMAN: Nostrils come in twos. Aachoo!

KIDNAPPER 2: Ooh! It's all over me!

WOMAN: Sorry! I'm not used to having it done to me.

KIDNAPPER 2: That's not what I've heard.

WOMAN: This isn't a Ray Cooney!

KIDNAPPER 2: Eh!

WOMAN: Ever thought of being an actor?

KIDNAPPER 2: What?

WOMAN: You're a natural... you know, when I was demonstrating those scenes.

KIDNAPPER 2: You think so? As a boy I... That's it! I'm going to tape up your mouth.

WOMAN: I've got a cold! it's torture! I'll keep quiet.

KIDNAPPER 2: OK, but you'll have to wear the blindfold.

WOMAN: Why?

KIDNAPPER 2: I want to take my mask off.

WOMAN: Before you do that I need to pee.

KIDNAPPER 2: What!

WOMAN: I need to urinate. Slash? Jimmy Riddle? Piss?

KIDNAPPER 2: Oh my god!

WOMAN: Alright! Don't panic, I've done it before. I take it you have a loo?

KIDNAPPER 2: Yes.

WOMAN: You'll have to take me.

KIDNAPPER 2: No... I don't think that's... no... it's a bit... no. No sorry. You'll just have to...

WOMAN: Come on! I've got tights on, if I wet myself, I'll get all itchy. Then I'll need some talc, I don't suppose you have any? Then it'll start dribbling down...

KIDNAPPER 2: Alright! Hang on, I'll loosen your ankles.

WOMAN: A bit more than that.

KIDNAPPER 2: There we are. [*She immediately starts shuffling up stage*] Where are you going? You can't piss in the fridge.

WOMAN: Well, how am I to know where kidnappers relieve themselves.

KIDNAPPER 2: It's over here. [*He helps her to the toilet*]

WOMAN: [*Almost at toilet door*] I need my hands free for my tights and pants.

KIDNAPPER 2: I'm not freeing your wrists.

WOMAN: Very well, you'll have to do it.

KIDNAPPER 2: Oh no!

WOMAN: Pull down my tights and panties...

KIDNAPPER 2: No really I couldn't... I just... No... I couldn't...

WOMAN: Come on don't be such a baby. Some men would jump at the chance.

KIDNAPPER 2: Well I won't. I mean don't er... I'm... I'm not like that.

WOMAN: Oh I see. You don't have to be embarrassed. I would have thought it would make it easier.

KIDNAPPER 2: What would?

WOMAN: Not liking women.

KIDNAPPER 2: I do like women.

WOMAN: Have you ever been intimate with a woman?

KIDNAPPER 2: Of course I bloody have! No it's not that. I'm not one of them. Er, not that there's anything wrong in... you know. Christ! No you've got it all wrong, no actually I'm a real Don June.

WOMAN: Juan!

KIDNAPPER 2: Well, all the time...

WOMAN: No! Don Juan. Have you a girl-friend?

KIDNAPPER 2: At this precise moment?... No, we've just split up.

WOMAN: Oh I'm sorry. What was her name?

KIDNAPPER 2: Michelle.

WOMAN: What was Michelle like?

KIDNAPPER 2: Stunning. Really good looking, a model... er intellectual too, you know, she was studying at night school, doing O-levels so she could go to college.

WOMAN: How did you meet?

KIDNAPPER 2: Her college, I was helping out with a modelling course, giving the girls tips...

WOMAN: Was she a good model?

KIDNAPPER 2: A bit shy at first, but we... er... worked at it.

WOMAN: Do you have many photos of Michelle?

KIDNAPPER 2: Fifty three - albums!

WOMAN: Did you sell any of them?

KIDNAPPER 2: Well, yes! To a couple of magazines.

WOMAN: We're not talking *Harpers & Queen*, are we?

KIDNAPPER 2: It was just harmless fun, providing a service for lonely...

WOMAN: Yes! Of course! Now, just imagine that I'm Michelle and your helping me get ready for... let's see... a photo session.

KIDNAPPER 2: I'll try!

WOMAN: That's right relax, keep imagining. An artistic pose perhaps?

KIDNAPPER 2: Artistic... yes! A fruit bowl! I know some really artistic things we could do with fruit.

WOMAN: I'm sure...

KIDNAPPER 2: [*Getting excited*] Oh... I'll get the soft filters and the muslin to drape over my 80mm Nikon...

WOMAN: Control yourself! That's men for you, give them a pair of panties to pull down and they lose their heads.

KIDNAPPER 2: It's stuck... er it's a bit tight.

WOMAN: Lift it! You hold, I'll wriggle.

KIDNAPPER 2: That's very good. I bet your excellent on a cat walk.

WOMAN: Now try.

KIDNAPPER 2: [*Reaches up and pulls down tights and pants*] Done it!

WOMAN: Well done!

KIDNAPPER 2: Thank you.

WOMAN: See what can be achieved by working together. Now, find me a small phillips electrical screwdriver.

KIDNAPPER 2: Right. What for?

WOMAN: Show a little sensitivity, did Michelle never ask you for one?

KIDNAPPER 2: Not that I can...

WOMAN: [*Whispering*] Women's things!

KIDNAPPER 2: Oh sorry! [*Goes to cupboard*]

WOMAN: [*Entering toilet*] There's no lock!

KIDNAPPER 2: Will this do? [*Holding small screwdriver*]

WOMAN: [*Taking it and disappearing into the loo*] Yes fine!

KIDNAPPER 2: Er... the door better stay open. [*Picking up his camera*]

WOMAN: You're not watching me!

KIDNAPPER 2: I mustn't take my lens... er... eyes off you.

WOMAN: In case I beat myself to death with the hair-dryer? Come on, close the door.

KIDNAPPER 2: No!

WOMAN: [*From inside*] I can't go if I'm being watched. I'm sure Michelle didn't let...

KIDNAPPER 2: Alright, I'll look the other way, but the door stays ajar.

WOMAN: I'm not going to make an escape down the cistern.

KIDNAPPER 2: [*Listening*] I can't hear any peeing.

WOMAN: Er... that's because you're listening. It's intimidating.

KIDNAPPER 2: Alright, I'll turn the TV on. [*Does so and sits in front of it fixing on a new lens to his camera*]

TV: And so the now agitated elephant calls across the jungle to her calf.

KIDNAPPER 2: *Wildlife on One.* [*The sound of an extraordinary volume of water sploshing down the loo. Satisfied he resumes watching the TV*]

WOMAN: [*Shuffles out of loo and stands provocatively by the door, but always keeping her hands by her side*] All done! I'm sorry to be a nuisance, I need you.

KIDNAPPER 2: Er... right. [*Pulls out his camera and starts flashing away*]

WOMAN: Not like this... I need to pose properly... I could lie on the bed... You were going to tell me what you can do with fruit...?

KIDNAPPER 2: [*Stops shooting*] Right! Passion fruit!

WOMAN: ...We could drape white sheets over it and you could slip a filter on to soften the focus...

KIDNAPPER 2: Oh yes! Mangos!

WOMAN: ...I'll lie here, you stand over me and shoot.

KIDNAPPER 2: Yes! Yes! Bananas! Yes!

WOMAN: Help me over to the bed.

KIDNAPPER 2: [*Puts the camera down and rips his shirt off*] Call me Don Joan.

[*He lunges at her. She produces electric wires in her hands and touches them against him, there is a flash. He is knocked over*]

KIDNAPPER 2: Oow! Bloody hell! What was that?

WOMAN: Electricity.

KIDNAPPER 2: Never happened to me before.

WOMAN: It's about to happen again. [*Puts wires against his chest*]

KIDNAPPER 2: Aaah! No! Stop.

WOMAN: The live and neutral from the hair-dryer. Strong stuff isn't it?

KIDNAPPER 2: I'm all pins and needles. I'm shaking.

WOMAN: Dirty little pervert! The big male weakness, your fucked up image of your sexuality. Crude male sexual fantasies... There's a lesson for you there, watch and learn. Contaaact! [*Gives him another shock*]

KIDNAPPER 2: Help! Bast... [*Writhing, his mask comes off*]

WOMAN: Oh dear, what a delinquent face!

KIDNAPPER 2: Bitch!

WOMAN: Lesson two, never insult someone who is holding live electrical wires four inches from your exposed nipples.

KIDNAPPER 2: Getting me all worked up, if I get hold of you...

WOMAN: Get hold of this. [*Touches the electrodes against his hands*]

KIDNAPPER 2: Ooouch! My hands... I can't move them!

WOMAN: How disconcerting, try rubbing them together.

KIDNAPPER 2: All the feelings gone... I'm polarised.

WOMAN: How about your legs?

KIDNAPPER 2: I can feel them.

WOMAN: Then try this! [*Connects wires to his legs*]

KIDNAPPER 2: Aaaah!

WOMAN: Can you move them, now?

KIDNAPPER 2: No... enough... please. Mercy!

WOMAN: Mercy, he asks for mercy! Weak-minded simpleton! You have manhandled me, chained me up, gagged me...

KIDNAPPER 2: I'm sorry, help me...

WOMAN: Shut up! I haven't finished! Blindfolded me, suffocated me and as a final humiliation were about to force me to live out your depraved fantasies. So don't insult my intelligence by asking for sympathy. Where are the keys to the padlock?

KIDNAPPER 2: I don't know!

WOMAN: You had them a minute ago.

KIDNAPPER 2: Yes, yes I did... in my hand... er... but when you shocked me I went like this... and they could've gone anywhere.

WOMAN: [*Taking off his shoes*] If you're going to lie, be convincing. Lesson three.

KIDNAPPER 2: It's true!

WOMAN: Alright! Let's hope it's not fatal. [*Puts wires on his feet*]

KIDNAPPER 2: Aaaah, no stop, I'll talk!

WOMAN: How disappointing, I expected a bigger jump.

KIDNAPPER 2: I can't move... I've got riga mortis...

WOMAN: Please, don't cry! It makes me very uncomfortable. If it's any consolation this is only a warm up for what I intend for Kevin. You're just suffering what's called shock paralysis.

KIDNAPPER 2: Help me! Do something.

WOMAN: You need an alcohol massage in the next half hour or you'll turn to jelly and probably die.

KIDNAPPER 2: I don't want to die.

WOMAN: Have you any alcohol?

KIDNAPPER 2: In the cupboard.

WOMAN: Key?

KIDNAPPER 2: In my pocket.

WOMAN: [*Getting it out*] Allow me.

KIDNAPPER 2: Hurry... I can hardly breathe.

WOMAN: Don't be so melodramatic. Suffer silently! [*Freeing chains*] Aaah! Liberty!

KIDNAPPER 2: Please, be quick, if you could, I beg of you.

WOMAN: What about that for manners? "Please". "If you could". I'm not a bitch or a cradle snatcher now am I?

KIDNAPPER 2: I'm sorry! Do something I'm going to pass out...

WOMAN: Don't do that! Come with me, that's right, we'll roll you on to the bed. [*Does so*]

KIDNAPPER 2: Hurry, I'm fading fast...

WOMAN: A proper prima donna; I'm going as fast as I can, all in good time.
    [*She starts chaining him to the bed*]

KIDNAPPER 2: What are you doing, I can't move anyway.

WOMAN: We've got chains, it's a pity not to use them. [*Gets scrubbing brush from the top of the fridge*] Ah just the job.

KIDNAPPER 2: What's it for?

WOMAN: Massage.

KIDNAPPER 2: A scrubbing brush?

WOMAN: Got to work in the alcohol. [*Going to cupboard*] Ah my ring. [*Looks for it*] Where's it gone?

KIDNAPPER 2: Don't know!

WOMAN: Bastards must've taken it! [*Holds up bottle of alcohol*] Not much left, I'll add some petrol.

KIDNAPPER 2: Petrol?

WOMAN: You have an attitude problem, there's no greater turn off than a negative attitude. A wonderful little cocktail of alcohol and petrol.

[*The telephone rings*]

Ah! your cronies. You're going to have to speak. I'll hold the phone in one hand and the electrodes in the other. Say the wrong thing, your eyes start playing pinball with your brain. [*Holding phone to his mouth*]

KIDNAPPER 2: Hullo, yes Tutti-frutti here... Yeah fine here... No problem... My voice?... Does it! Oh that's probably because I'm lying down... Well because I'm feeling so... loose. How're things with you... Have you got the "present"? Oh it's still in the "shop"... How long before I see you? [*Panic-stricken*] An hour and a half, can't you make it sooner? [*She clouts him*] No fine!... Yes, yes all chained up... OK bye. [*Takes phone away*] I think I'm going to cry.

WOMAN: I've told you about that before. You did well! To the massage! [*Puts shirt over his face*] That'll keep the spray out of your eyes, let's give you a good scrubbing.

KIDNAPPER 2: Ah! You're skinning me!

WOMAN: That attitude again.

KIDNAPPER 2: I can move my fingers.

WOMAN: I told you, it's my scrubbing.

KIDNAPPER 2: [*Grabbing WOMAN's wrists*] Aah! Got you!

WOMAN: Get off!

KIDNAPPER 2: I've got you! You're going to be sorry you ever pissed me around.

WOMAN: Ow! Lesson four - don't jump to hasty conclusions.

KIDNAPPER 2: I'm not going to listen to a wor...

WOMAN: You're covered in petrol and alcohol... So one spark and you're kidnapper flambé.

KIDNAPPER 2: How do you intend to make a spark? [*WOMAN takes out lighter*] Oh shit!

WOMAN: Let's see! [*Lights it*] There we are! God always helps financiers in a fix. Your fifth and most important lesson, always keep something back. A contingency.

KIDNAPPER 2: Please...

WOMAN: Unless you return to a prostrate position immediately, I drop the lighter on to your greasy body.

KIDNAPPER 2: [*Lying down*] Mrs McKaye, please, don't flambé me... Please no more... Don't hurt me... I can't take any more pain.

WOMAN: Stop whining! You were sprightly enough a minute ago. [*Takes his socks off*] This should stop you getting ideas, I'll attach the wires to your halluces.

KIDNAPPER 2: No please, I want to have children.

WOMAN: Your big toes are halluces.

KIDNAPPER 2: Oh my halluces.

WOMAN: One false move, I plug you into the national grid.

KIDNAPPER 2: Monster! A rich, ruthless, capitalist monster feeding on ordinary simple people.

WOMAN: Thank you Karl Marx! Whilst I prepare you for the oven you better tell me all about your colleagues, or you'll be roasted.

KIDNAPPER 2: I'll tell you! Ask me anything!

WOMAN: Where are we?

KIDNAPPER 2: Farnham in Surrey near Guildford.

WOMAN: North Downs?

KIDNAPPER 2: Not far from the A3.

WOMAN: Your associates, their names and where they're from!

KIDNAPPER 2: They'll kill me and my family.

WOMAN: I see, in that case a difficult decision. I believe in freedom of choice so I'll leave it to you to decide. I'll just explain what I'm going to do to you, listen very carefully, it's important you understand the implications. Are you concentrating?

KIDNAPPER 2: Yes go ahead.

WOMAN: I'm going to set light to you and then I'll stand just here with a fire extinguisher, when you agree to talk I put you out! Er... have you made your decision?

KIDNAPPER 2: The Chief used to write on the Independent then he moved to BBC Radio 4 but was made redund...

WOMAN: I don't want their CV's. Just names and addresses. [*Hands him pad and pen*] Write them down, while I pop this rope around your neck.

KIDNAPPER 2: Christ! You're going to hang me.

WOMAN: Get a grip! It's just to stop you reaching down and fiddling with the electrodes.

KIDNAPPER 2: But I wouldn't dream...

WOMAN: Silence, liar! [*Tugs the rope*]

KIDNAPPER 2: You're strangling me.

WOMAN: Good, it works. [*Takes the paper back*] Thank you! Now to delicately extract the vital piece of information...

KIDNAPPER 2: I'll tell you anything!

WOMAN: Who is the insider, your boss? The middle-man!

KIDNAPPER 2: I really don't know anything about that.

WOMAN: [*Picks up the plug*] I want a name.

KIDNAPPER 2: I can't...!

WOMAN: You are prepared to take responsibility for your decision, I respect that. Three seconds to change your mind - or it's bonfire time. One...

KIDNAPPER 2: Help! Police, anyone help!

WOMAN: Two...

KIDNAPPER 2: Honestly! I don't know... Oh God!

WOMAN: Three. [*Plugging in, a huge explosion, flame and smoke*]

KIDNAPPER 2: Ow! Stop it!

WOMAN: The name?

KIDNAPPER 2: It's your lover!

WOMAN: Which one?

KIDNAPPER 2: The suit!

WOMAN: Willoughby?

KIDNAPPER 2: Yes!

WOMAN: [*Unplugs him*] I don't believe it, it can't be! [*Squirts him with the fire extinguisher*]

KIDNAPPER 2: I've been cremated!

WOMAN: I'm destroyed. Oh snookums, my baby snookums how could you?

KIDNAPPER 2: [*Singing*] "Open now the crystal fountain, whence the healing stream doth flow".

WOMAN: Sssh! [*Sprays him*] My only true love, almost my son, my protegé, my own sweet PR man. Why did you tell me? Bastard!

KIDNAPPER 2: "Let the cloud and fiery pillars lead me all my journey through".

WOMAN: [*Squirts him again*] Snookums, I would've given you anything, You do this to me! Break my heart! For a million.

KIDNAPPER 2: "Bread of heaven, bread of heaven, lead me now and ever more".

WOMAN: Quiet! [*Another squirt*] The deceit! I loved him, chose him to rescue me. How could he... I've been used I can't bear it... I want to die!

KIDNAPPER 2: [*Covered in foam*] It's all gone white I'm in the clouds! Oh look! Angels, sirens, heavenly muses! Smile for the camera! I'm flying, I can see everything. It's snowing on Christmas day, England are in the World cup, the Tories have lost an election. Yes! I'm going to heaven...

WOMAN: I can't bear it! [*Slumps onto KIDNAPPER 2*]

KIDNAPPER 2: Ow! It hurts!

WOMAN: The pain!

KIDNAPPER 2: The agony!

WOMAN & KIDNAPPER 2: [*Scream*]

□

ACT TWO

The same scene a few minutes later.

[KIDNAPPER 2 is lying prostrate centre stage. WOMAN enters with bottle of whisky and tumbler]

WOMAN: How could he do it to me? How could he? [*Kicking KIDNAPPER 2*] I said how could he! [*He moans*] For what? A million! I would have given him it, even index-linked the repayments. Why? [*Kicking KIDNAPPER 2 again*] Do you have any idea what that man meant to me? You know he had little pet-names for me "Wiggly-bum" and "Goebals", now look he's driven me to supermarket scotch.

KIDNAPPER 2: Ah! Be still my wings, for I have arrived.

WOMAN: I used to say "He was my only true wealth". Ha! It shows how easily even I can be manipulated. Well that's it! No more soft-touch for me. There's a lesson here for all of us, particularly you. [*Kicking him again*] Always look after number one, trust nobody, the only honest motive is the self and self-gratification. Get up!

KIDNAPPER 2: Please let me enter. Though I was a photo-journalist I repent.

WOMAN: I've learnt my lesson! No more sentimentality...

KIDNAPPER 2: Here! Re-string this harp for me would you?

WOMAN: If I want something I take it, regardless of who...

KIDNAPPER 2: Pleased to meet you Santa. I'm looking for Benny Hill.

WOMAN: He made my public image... arranged that appearance on *Through the Keyhole*...

KIDNAPPER 2: I'll have another pint of nectar.

WOMAN: Will you stop your cretinous dribbling, you're ruining a perfectly good speech.

KIDNAPPER 2: [*Seeing her*] Ah! I'm in the other place. Keep away Lucifer...

WOMAN: [*Throwing tumbler of whisky in his face*] This isn't *Faust*!

KIDNAPPER 2: Ow, that stings! Ow my burns!

WOMAN: That's brought you down to earth.

KIDNAPPER 2: The Devil! That's who you are! Come for my soul.

WOMAN: A dramatic persecution complex! Too much Shakespeare in your formative years.

KIDNAPPER 2: I'm one great blister, look at me.

WOMAN: Don't make such a fuss. Second degree burn at most. You'll survive! All we need is a little oil.

KIDNAPPER 2: You're going to burn me alive!

WOMAN: Omit Shakespeare insert Wagner! Olive oil to soothe burns.

KIDNAPPER 2: Thank you!

WOMAN: Enlightened self-interest. I have a score to settle with snookums for...

KIDNAPPER 2: Cashing in his assets?

WOMAN: [*Tugging on rope*] Peasant! How dare you make light of my relationship. He is an Adonis, and in the sexuality department he's a long way past readers' wives. [*Looking in the fridge*] Might've known you plebs wouldn't run to olive oil. We'll make do with the double chocolate fudge.

KIDNAPPER 2: Ice-cream?

WOMAN: That's right. Just the job. Here goes! And bear in mind I still have a lighter and the rope. [*Rubbing*] Arms up! He came from one of the best families. From Newcastle.

KIDNAPPER 2: That's a contradiction in terms. Ow! The pain!

WOMAN: This year's stock exchange ball he dressed as one of those homeless people - complete with dog it was so amusing.

KIDNAPPER 2: [*Still rubbing*] Sounds like a merchant banker.

WOMAN: He used to be.

KIDNAPPER 2: A lucky guess. Ouch!

WOMAN: [*Stopping*] How he could do it?

KIDNAPPER 2: It's what you expect in the City.

WOMAN: [*Goes back to rubbing*] There you are, better?

KIDNAPPER 2: A little; let's talk some more about snookums.

WOMAN: Oh no you don't! Keeping me talking so your comrades can come back and blow my brains out.

KIDNAPPER 2: They wouldn't do a thing like that. I should be in intensive care.

WOMAN: Shut up! [*Picking up phone*] I need a little help, let's see... the number.

KIDNAPPER 2: You're calling the police? Good idea! Tell them to bring an ambulance.

WOMAN: I am calling my mother.

KIDNAPPER 2: Your mother? The one who conceived you? Gave birth to you?

WOMAN: What is this *Roget's Thesaurus*?

KIDNAPPER 2: What manner of creature is she?

WOMAN: [*Tugging the rope*] My mother is a wonderful, sweet person... if a little... eccentric! Slightly off the wall! Completely round the twist. Ah! Mother, how are you?

[*MOTHER appears on the phone; a split scene*]

MOTHER: Who is it?

WOMAN: What do you mean, who is it? It's Diana.

MOTHER: Diana? I know at least six Dianas... Which one?

WOMAN: Mother! Your daughter.

MOTHER: Why didn't you say so? Your voice is so different on the phone!... Ah! I was trying to get hold of you. I can't find that little portable television you gave me when we got married.

WOMAN: When you got married, I wasn't around, neither was portable television.

MOTHER: Really? How did we used to watch the news then?

WOMAN: Mother... I'm calling you because...

MOTHER: You know I can't find those red shoes with the black heels either. Vanished! If you ask me it's the spirits.

WOMAN: Listen! [*To KIDNAPPER 2, tugging on rope*] Keep still!

MOTHER: Sorry dear! It's the chair, I must get it re-upholstered.

WOMAN: Mother, I've been made off with!

MOTHER: Made off with? Wonderful! Who by? Anyone I know? Who is this madman on the loose?

WOMAN: It's not a question of sex.

MOTHER: Pity! What is it a question of then?

WOMAN: Have you read the papers today?

MOTHER: Ooh. Yes! I was... dying...

WOMAN: Well be quick then...

MOTHER: What?

WOMAN: Tell me!

MOTHER: No, dear you phoned me.

WOMAN: What you were dying to tell me?

MOTHER: Not dying... dying! Everywhere people dying! Wars, bombs, rail crashes, road crashes! In Europe, Africa, America... they're even dying in Australia now. I don't know what's happening. In my day that sort of thing never happened to foreigners.

WOMAN: Never mind that! The front page of your *Telegraph* there's news of an abduction. Did you see it?

MOTHER: Oh no! I always avoid the salacious stories, they upset me... It's too like one of your papers, I always think "what if it happened to one of the family".

WOMAN: Mother! It has happened!

MOTHER: What! Who?

WOMAN: Me! I've been kidnapped!

MOTHER: Diana, don't be so silly... If you've been kidnapped what are you doing chatting away down the phone?

WOMAN: I've freed myself!

MOTHER: My god! You talk like all those feminists used to: freed yourself indeed.

WOMAN: It's true! I was kidnapped but then they left me alone with one crook who tried to lay his hands on me.

MOTHER: Ooh, hands on you, in what sense?

WOMAN: I'll tell you all the details when I see you.

MOTHER: No no, tell me now... Hang on I'll just grab a cushion and a cigarette. What an adventure! OK go ahead, what's he like then this crook?

WOMAN: Never mind now, I'm in a hurry!

MOTHER: You spend your life generating scandal, up to your neck in filth and once in a blue moon when you ring, you're in too much of a hurry to tell your old mother a good tale of violence and passion.

WOMAN: Mother! For heavens sake! Come here straight away. [*KIDNAPPER 2 moans*]

MOTHER: Diana what's got into you?

WOMAN: [*To KIDNAPPER 2*] Be quiet or I'll string you up.

MOTHER: Hang your own mother? Diana, it's true what they say about you.

WOMAN: No, that was someone else. Take the car and come here straight away.

MOTHER: Don't you take that "independent business-woman" tone with me my girl.

WOMAN: Yes mother I'm sorry, just listen. Get in the car, take the A3, go to Guildford, it shouldn't take more than twenty minutes.

MOTHER: OK and where are you?

WOMAN: Hang on, he can explain it to you himself. [*To KIDNAP-PER 2, tugging rope*] Speak nicely to my mother and tell her how to get here. [*Hands over the receiver*]

KIDNAPPER 2: Good afternoon to you, madam.

MOTHER: Hello dear... Oh what a lovely voice... Well?

KIDNAPPER 2: About three miles before Guildford you'll pass Gravel Quarry Reservoir. Take the track on the left past the land-fill sight. You'll come to a sign saying "Lakeside Enterprise Centre - Executive Suites for Entrepreneurs". There are three corrugated iron huts, behind them an abandoned factory with a pink ice cream cone on top. We're there.

MOTHER: How romantic.

WOMAN: [*Taking back the receiver*] Did you get all that mother?

MOTHER: Hasn't he got a lovely deep voice. You can tell he's the passionate type!

WOMAN: Mother! I want you to go up to the gun room, get out the first and the third in the rack, the shot guns. Don't forget to bring the cartridges, two boxes for each gun. Oh and a hacksaw.

MOTHER: But my dear surely you have no intention of...

WOMAN: Mother that's enough!

MOTHER: I'll be right there! [*Hanging up*] Murderess!
[*Exits*]

WOMAN: Good she should be here in half an hour!

KIDNAPPER 2: Quicker on the broomstick.

WOMAN: That does it, one more of your imbecilic observations about my family and I am plugging you in.

KIDNAPPER 2: [*Really going for it*] No you can't, I'm dying as it is. See what you've done to me? My insides are burning, my outsides are burning, the fire has spread to my brain so that all I can think about is death. Look at me, I'm dying. Help me! "Tis too horrible, the weariest and most loathed worldly life that age ache penury and imprisonment can lay on nature is a paradise to what we fear of death. Sweet sister let me live".

WOMAN: [*She has been clearing out the fridge*] Get in!

KIDNAPPER 2: What!

WOMAN: The fridge, I've prepared it for you.

KIDNAPPER 2: Oh right! Thank you! Why?

WOMAN: Keep you cool. Pop in! It'll be just like Captain Scott in his igloo.

KIDNAPPER 2: The burning will go away?

WOMAN: Of course! Cold is an anaesthetic. Make yourself comfortable.

KIDNAPPER 2: Can you take the chains off and the electrodes...

WOMAN: Certainly not! I'm alone and defenceless.

KIDNAPPER 2: Defenceless!

WOMAN: Sit there! If there are no more dramatics you can watch the television. [*Handing it over*] The remote control.

KIDNAPPER 2: Thank you! It's quite comfortable.

[*A PRIEST enters top of the stairs*]

PRIEST: [*Speaking to someone off stage*] Alright, wait there. Stay on that sofa, and don't play with your thurible.

WOMAN: Who the hell! [*Closing fridge door*] My God!

PRIEST: Very close! Just a little clerical joke. I am the vicar madam... Er, we were doing the rounds... as it were... I hope you don't mind...

WOMAN: Who were you talking to?

PRIEST: Ah now, that's my Altar Boy. He's up in reception, if that's alright with you. Actually he's more a trainee altar boy, he's on work experience. Very keen but rather shy and nervous and with a tendency to hallucinate what with the stories about this place...

WOMAN: What stories?

PRIEST: You know people are terribly superstitious and what with the place being empty...

WOMAN: Yes I'm here... on holiday.

PRIEST: You should lock the doors. One has to be careful what with all the goings on nowadays.

WOMAN: You're telling me!

PRIEST: I wouldn't have chosen this as a holiday home.

WOMAN: Smell the fresh air listen to the sound of bird song, the breeze rustling leaves and...

[*KIDNAPPER 2 moans from fridge*]

PRIEST: What was that?

WOMAN: Rustling leaves!

PRIEST: Oh!... [*Listening*] Tortured souls!

WOMAN: What!

PRIEST: Well, I'm not one for spreading gossip. [*Pulling up a chair*] May I? It was a terrible tragedy. A young lad worked here as an assistant pasteuriser. He loved the job, addicted to maple and pecan surprise, he was. When he got his redundancy notice, he went quite crazy, gathered the entire workforce in this room, turned the lights out and shot every last one of them. Naturally, people say that their anguished souls now wander the factory.

WOMAN: People do believe such crap Reverend?

PRIEST: Yes complete cra... nonsense, of course. But I must admit that a moment ago when walking past I thought I heard cries, moans... [*Pointing upstairs*] The boy heard them too.

WOMAN: Ah that'll be the television. They show some terribly violent films; if I had any children I'd worry about them. Rape, abduction, reconstructions of violent crimes, Jeremy Beadle...
[*KIDNAPPER 2 moans*]

PRIEST: Listen to that! it's coming from in the room.

WOMAN: Uh... What's your view on the ordination of women...
[*More moans*]

PRIEST: Can't you hear it?

WOMAN: What's that?
[*KIDNAPPER 2 wails*]

PRIEST: There it is again, a sort of wailing.

WOMAN: That's the fridge.

PRIEST: A wailing fridge?

WOMAN: No! Don't open it!

PRIEST: [*Throwing the door open*] Holy shit!

WOMAN: Reverend!

PRIEST: Sorry! It's a... There's a man in here.

KIDNAPPER 2: Air! Give me air.

WOMAN: Yes, that's right.

PRIEST: But, who is he?

WOMAN: My husband.

PRIEST: Your husband?

WOMAN: Yes.

PRIEST: You keep him in the fridge?

WOMAN: That's right.

PRIEST: Is that normal?

WOMAN: Perfectly! He's in training, five minute stints at first and then gradually increasing. Unfortunately you interrupted him with twenty seconds to go.

PRIEST: [*Slamming fridge door on him*] I'm so sorry.

WOMAN: You see, he can simulate Kilimanjaro in there... right up to twenty seven thousand feet.

PRIEST: Your husband's a climber...?

WOMAN: That's right!

PRIEST: But he's in chains!

WOMAN: Yes... Snow chains.

PRIEST: But...

WOMAN: Ah! [*Throwing open door*] Time's up! Five minutes.

KIDNAPPER 2: Help me, vicar, call an ambulance, the police, anyone. I can't stand any more!

WOMAN: Altitude sickness...

PRIEST: He's all covered in blisters...

WOMAN: Oh! Yes... The glare of the glaciers at that height, no joke and I'm afraid he refuses to put on his ice cream, don't you dear?

PRIEST: Ice cream?

KIDNAPPER 2: St. Peter! Please! Do something. Lucifer is winning.

PRIEST: Oh dear!

WOMAN: Don't worry darling, we'll help you. [*Taking PRIEST aside*] You've discovered our secret. He has a terrible persecution complex. I don't why!

PRIEST: Poor fellow!

WOMAN: That's why he trains himself to scale inaccessible peaks, he believes that up there nobody will be able to get at him.

PRIEST: I understand madam! Of course, in the long run, your husband is only running away from himself. No amount of Everests will save us if we cannot find peace within ourselves.

WOMAN: How true!

KIDNAPPER 2: Save me! I've been tortured by a bastard business woman, a female media exploiter, an oppressor, a city she-monster, a rich she-devil. Lucifer is a woman.

PRIEST: Who are these people?

WOMAN: No idea!

PRIEST: Do I detect a note of misogyny?

WOMAN: He was bottle fed!

KIDNAPPER 2: I confess I have sinned, I am a criminal, I kidnapped her even attempted to molest her... I deserve life... call the police! Save me!

PRIEST: See how he takes the sins of the world onto his shoulders.

WOMAN: He has an almost mystical desire for expiation.

PRIEST: He certainly is a serious case.

WOMAN: Call me a sentimental fool, vicar, but I can't let them shut him up, abuse and institutionalise him in one of those hospitals with pills and electric shocks. [*To KIDNAPPER 2, tugging rope*] Don't touch those wires!

PRIEST: What are those things attached to his halluces?

WOMAN: Electrodes! So I can let him have a little dose every now and again.

KIDNAPPER 2: Don't listen to her, she's killing me. She is the criminal. She runs the media.

PRIEST: That's a bit strong! Classic reversal from the prostration-guilt syndrome to pure aggression. Is he a socialist?

WOMAN: It's not that bad! [*To KIDNAPPER 2*] Time for a rest, darling! [*Slams fridge door*] Ten minutes on Kilimanjaro should calm you down.

PRIEST: Isn't he in danger of suffocating?

WOMAN: Not seriously. He holds his breath and goes into a sort of nirvana.

PRIEST: Anaerobic nirvana?

WOMAN: Absolutely, it's marvellous what you can achieve when you're completely potty. Would you believe, he's convinced a devil has taken control of him.

PRIEST: Yes I would! Why do you say it with such scepticism?

WOMAN: Come now, it's medieval superstition...

PRIEST: Madam, you shouldn't dismiss the Devil as superstition.

WOMAN: Do you think my husband is possessed?

PRIEST: It could well be! Even the new Archbishop, after all...

WOMAN: Is possessed by the devil?

PRIEST: That's right... No, certainly not! But he's convinced that he exists...

WOMAN: So he should be!

PRIEST: ...And is responsible for so much madness among men...

WOMAN: The Archbishop?

PRIEST: The Devil! If you knew how many strange forms of dementia have been routed out by a single prayer. I myself...

WOMAN: [*Taking him over to the fridge*] Vicar, could you exorcise my fridge... husband?

PRIEST: Now? Right here?

WOMAN: Yes! If you don't have to rush off. I'd be terribly grateful

PRIEST: Very well! I'll try! [*Going to stairs*] I need a few odds and ends. I can't guarantee anything. [*Calling off*] I need the holy water. [*Hip-flask is thrown downstairs and the PRIEST takes swig*]

WOMAN: [*Opening fridge door to whisper to KIDNAPPER 2*] Any more histrionics... the door shuts and in goes the plug.

PRIEST: [*Calling*] Candle!

[*Candle and box of matches are thrown to him*]

KIDNAPPER 2: You're growing horns and a pointy tail.

WOMAN: Shhh!

PRIEST: And the thurible. [*It is thrown to him*] Thank you Rupert. [*The PRIEST holds up the candle then kneels down in front of the WOMAN, shuts the fridge door, puts down the candle and starts waving the thurible*]

WOMAN: What are you doing? It's not me that needs exorcising.

PRIEST: I need you to be the medium. Now put your hands on me just here.

[*Diana's MOTHER enters carrying a shot gun*]

MOTHER: Diana! Where are you? Goodness! What a lot of smoke.

WOMAN: Ah! Mother at last, come in. This is Reverend...

PRIEST: Er... Oscar O' Flaherty, pleased to meet you.

MOTHER: The gangster! You can tell by the eyes, and a member of the clergy too. Well, my dear I really wasn't expecting this! Vicars, sex, drugs...

WOMAN: Mother...

MOTHER: ...It's like one of your newspapers. I'd heard that you fabricate the stories but I didn't know you did the dirty work yourself.

PRIEST: Madam...!

MOTHER: I can see what's been going on - even with these glasses! I am a broad-minded person, as you know...

WOMAN: Mother, he was just preparing me for a medium job.

MOTHER: Well, I've heard it called a lot of foul names, but that's a new one on me!

PRIEST: Do you have something against the clergy?

MOTHER: Not as long as they limit themselves to their clerical duties.

WOMAN: We were preparing for the exorcism, to flush the devil out of his stomach.

MOTHER: And what's wrong with Alkaseltzer? If only your husband knew what...

PRIEST: But we are doing it for him, to bring him out of himself.

MOTHER: [*Pointing gun at him*] Watch your step! Make a joke of it indeed...

WOMAN: [*Seeing the shot gun*] Oh well done Mother. Did you bring the cartridges and hacksaw as well?

PRIEST: I feel I must inform you that I'm a paid up member of The League Against Blood Sports.

WOMAN: Don't worry, we won't be shooting wildlife.

PRIEST: What will you be shooting at...?

MOTHER: Priests!

WOMAN: Mother!

MOTHER: Particularly those who specialise in tactile exorcisms with married women. [*Again pointing the gun at him*]

WOMAN: [*Taking gun*] Don't worry Reverend, she's a little odd but she means well.

MOTHER: Diana! The fridge is no place to keep bits of rope. [*Opening fridge*] Or human bodies. Oh my god! Who is it?

WOMAN: Surely you recognise him, he's my husband.

MOTHER: Heavens! These lenses are worse than I thought. How strange he looks.

WOMAN: [*Pulling rope*] Say hullo to mother, darling.

KIDNAPPER 2: Alright there mum... How's things?

MOTHER: Stranger and stranger! These glasses even distort peoples voices.

WOMAN: Where is the other gun?

MOTHER: I rested it on the display in reception.

WOMAN: What display?

MOTHER: The statue of the young boy lying naked on a sofa, his body covered in ice cream...

PRIEST: That was no statue, that's Rupert.

MOTHER: Rupert?

WOMAN: The altar boy.
[*She goes upstairs*]

PRIEST: He's a little shy.

WOMAN: He's gone!

PRIEST: Don't worry, he's a good boy. They think the world of him at his remand home.

WOMAN: Remand home! The boy is too shy to show his face, he has a tendency to hallucinate, he lies naked in reception, covered in ice cream pretending to be a statue...

MOTHER: He's obviously deranged!

WOMAN: Now he's running round the countryside with a shot gun.
[*She exits*]

PRIEST: Rupert wouldn't hurt a fly. Now let's see, I'm going to have to ask you to act as the medium. [*Sitting mother in chair*] Now do you believe in demons.

WOMAN: One look at you is enough to convince anyone, Reverend.

PRIEST: Please refrain from making light of it, and concentrate. [*Taking her hands*] I need to see if you have the necessary spirit.

MOTHER: Spirit me? I light lamps with it!

PRIEST: [*A gun shot is heard*] What an exceptional reaction, we'll get that demon.

MOTHER: What demon?

PRIEST: The one that's made it's way through your son-in-law's mouth into his stomach.

MOTHER: Impossible!

PRIEST: What is?

MOTHER: That any demon, however ingenious, could manage to infiltrate his stomach. Diana's husband barely stops talking long enough to digest food let alone devils. Mind you he had a very strange up-bringing... but I mustn't gossip.

PRIEST: Madam really, I must insist...

MOTHER: Very well then! His great uncle...

PRIEST: Try to concentrate on the matter in hand. Do you know the *Memori Exum Inferi.*

MOTHER: Certainly I do!

PRIEST: Good, then sing it to the fridge. In A minor. Go - *vigelibus enixae equaminus memori exum ad inferi venimus.*

[*KIDNAPPERS enter wearing their masks, CHIEF is hand cuffed to an attache case. YOUNG MAN is wearing the Thatcher mask*]

MOTHER: Oh my God! Reverend, you were right. What faces! Devils!

PRIEST: Keep singing... *Benimus in laude.*

CHIEF KIDNAPPER: Who are you?

YOUNG MAN: What are they doing?

KIDNAPPER 3: Shall I smack 'um?

MOTHER: Out, out vile creatures! *Utque fuerunt.*

YOUNG MAN: I think that's Latin.

PRIEST: [*Shaking the thurible*] *Exum adium ad inferi.*

KIDNAPPER 3: Leave it to me Chief! [*Grabbing PRIEST*] Listen I don't like Latiners, especially when they carry smoke bombs and wear dresses.

YOUNG MAN: He's a Priest.

KIDNAPPER 3: [*Dropping him*] Why didn't someone tell me!

CHIEF KIDNAPPER: Where are they?

KIDNAPPER 3: Your reverence, would you happen to have seen a man wearing a mask like ours?

PRIEST: A masked man? Certainly not!

CHIEF KIDNAPPER: And the woman?

PRIEST: Masked too, was she?

KIDNAPPER 3: No tied up and gagged.

MOTHER: You've been watching too many westerns.

PRIEST: No, haven't seen her.

CHIEF KIDNAPPER: Christ! That moron has let her escape.

YOUNG MAN: Look, the fridge is moving.

CHIEF KIDNAPPER: It could be a trick.

KIDNAPPER 3: Stand back, I'm going to shoot.

MOTHER: No, for pity sake it's my daughter's husband!

CHIEF KIDNAPPER: Your daughter married a refrigerator?

MOTHER: No she married a prick! But he swallowed a devil and now he's in the fridge.

YOUNG MAN: I understand Chief! They're nutters, escaped lunatics. He thinks he's a Priest and she's a witch.

MOTHER: Who are you calling a witch?

PRIEST: [*Pointing*] We're just preparing to exorcise it.

CHIEF KIDNAPPER: The fridge?

PRIEST: The devil inside her son-in-law, who's inside the fridge, simulating Kilimanjaro.

CHIEF KIDNAPPER: That's our fridge. [*Opening the fridge door*] It's you! What the hell...

KIDNAPPER 2: I'm up to thirty thousand feet, no oxygen... and I'm fighting the Devil within, and the devil without - who's a woman. Just as well I've got these snow chains...

KIDNAPPER 3: He's been at the funny stuff! Have you been smoking?

KIDNAPPER 2: Smoking... yes! Burning... yes! Petrol massage... yes! Not that I'm complaining, not with these electrodes on my toes. I know what happens when I complain; the McKaye devil stuffs the plug into the nearest socket and up I go like Guy Fawkes.

CHIEF KIDNAPPER: Where is McKaye?

KIDNAPPER 2: Stoking the furnace of Hades. [*Shuts himself in fridge*]

MOTHER: If you are speaking about my daughter, she is disarming an altar boy.

PRIEST: Let's get on with the exorcism... *Gloria si fuerunt mali.*

KIDNAPPER 3: [*To PRIEST*] You're a nutter, so shut up!

CHIEF KIDNAPPER: [*Sinking into a chair*] Why can't something I touch go right! Mad priests, altar boys with guns, colleagues who have taken to living in fridges. I can't cope!

KIDNAPPER 3: [*To PRIEST*] Look what you've done, you've upset the Chief.

YOUNG MAN: No need to panic, we may have lost McKaye, but we've gained her mother.

KIDNAPPER 2: [*Opening fridge door*] That's not much of a bargain.

MOTHER: [*To KIDNAPPER 2*] Listen, pillock, quite apart from the fact that I realise - even with these glasses on - you're not my son-in-law, that's the second time you've insulted me, the next time will be your last.

CHIEF KIDNAPPER: Gag her! Take the chains off that jerk and use them to tie up the vicar.

KIDNAPPER 3: [*With YOUNG MAN getting chains off KIDNAPPER 2*] Hey! Get his camera and we're back on with our insurance policy. [*Pointing to MOTHER*] A shot of her with the Priest in chains.

YOUNG MAN: [*Chaining PRIEST*] "McKaye's mum manacles minister".

KIDNAPPER 3: You're learning! How about "Screwing ministers - the family business".

CHIEF KIDNAPPER: Never mind that! We've got to find that cheating son of... daughter of a bitch, criminal, corrupt city... ruthless rich bastard... exploiting... bastard.

MOTHER: You are alluding to my Diana! We have not been introduced nor had any personal dealings; so let me tell you I am the afore mentioned mother! OK? Cowardly prick!

CHIEF KIDNAPPER: Now all and sundry start calling me a prick. [*To KIDNAPPER 2*] It's all thanks to you.

KIDNAPPER 2: It's not my fault! She said she wanted to go to the toilet, she did too, you could hear it, "psspsss" it was louder than the tv, the elephants were trumpeting across the savannah "whaaaooo" but you could still hear it "psspss". I had to pull 'em down and then up and what with the soft focus and the fruit... I wanted to...

YOUNG MAN: Give her one!

PRIEST: Now, now! A little respect for the mother at least.

KIDNAPPER 2: There were the shocks that burned my insides, the petrol that burnt my outside, the rope around my neck, the scrubbing brush, I was attacked by devils... But I have seen heaven! I've reformed! I'll no longer pedal the establishment's inane sensationalist garbage that subdues and emasculates our people.

KIDNAPPER 3: You're going to work for *The Mirror*?

KIDNAPPER 2: I'm going to work for the cause...

YOUNG MAN: *The Morning Star*?

KIDNAPPER 2: A better life...

CHIEF KIDNAPPER: *The Independent*?

KIDNAPPER 2: I devote my life to exposing the establishment, the corrupt ruling classes and most of all that evil bloodsucking, inhuman whore of a...

MOTHER: That really is enough! I warned you! [*Plugging him in*] Take that!

KIDNAPPER 2: Aaah! [*Sings*] "Guide me O thou great Jehovah, pilgrim through this barren land..."

CHIEF KIDNAPPER: The plug. Take it out!

[*KIDNAPPER 3 does so*]

KIDNAPPER 2: She attached the wires to my halluces.

KIDNAPPER 3: Poor sod! You wanted children.

KIDNAPPER 2: Help me back to my fridge.

CHIEF KIDNAPPER: I'm the one who's been got, chained to this.

KIDNAPPER 3: And not an oxygen torch in miles.

[*WOMAN appears at top of stairs*]

WOMAN: I have returned to free you from your chains.

KIDNAPPER 3: It's her... get her!

[*They go for her, she produces a shot gun*]

WOMAN: One more step and it's kidnapper pie! When will you learn?

MOTHER: Brilliant Diana! I knew you'd turn up! My daughter's better than the seventh cavalry! She always comes!

[*YOUNG MAN sniggers*]

WOMAN & MOTHER: Shut up!

CHIEF KIDNAPPER: Quick! We'll use her as a shield.

[*CHIEF, KIDNAPPER 3 hide behind MOTHER and YOUNG MAN darts behind PRIEST*]

KIDNAPPER 2: My fridge is bullet proof. So there!

CHIEF KIDNAPPER: See if she has the courage to shoot her own mother.

MOTHER: Fools you don't know the McKayes.

KIDNAPPER 3: [*Holding pistol*] One false move! *Hasta la vista*, Baby!

WOMAN: Well, of course it's your choice...

KIDNAPPER 2: [*Shutting fridge door*] I've heard this before. You're done for.

WOMAN: If you choose to put down your guns, I have the combination. We could get the money. If not, I will undoubtedly splatter your innards all over the audience. Sorry mother, unfortunately that would have to include you. No hard feelings?

MOTHER: Not at all dear! In your position I'd have blown the bastards to buggery by now.

CHIEF KIDNAPPER: How do we know it's not one of your tricks?

WOMAN: Have I deceived you up to now?

CHIEF KIDNAPPER: Look at the state of him. [*Pointing to fridge*] He was perfectly sane when we left.

KIDNAPPER 3: I think that's pushing it a bit, Chief.

WOMAN: Natural wastage - it's a tough business - have to get rid of the dead wood. Besides it was self-defence.

CHIEF KIDNAPPER: We don't even know if the cash is in there.

WOMAN: Incompetents! You didn't check?

KIDNAPPER 2: [*Opening fridge door*] Huh! The incompetence!

CHIEF KIDNAPPER: Well it was like you said. [*Pointing to YOUNG MAN*] He went in on his own.

WOMAN: Move aside vicar!

[*He does so revealing YOUNG MAN in Thatcher mask*]

There you are! Snookums how could you! I know you're the brains behind the whole thing. You dared to play the lover with me. You're going to pay for it!

MOTHER: Diana you can't murder all your unfaithful lovers. It'd be a blood-bath.

WOMAN: So you intended to walk away with my money?

MOTHER: I always said that he was no good, dear. Shoot him.

CHIEF KIDNAPPER: [*To KIDNAPPER 3*] She thinks he's Willoughby, her PR man.

YOUNG MAN: [*On his knees*] No please! I didn't want to come back! They made me! I'm on your side really, my name isn't Snookums or Kevin and... I love you!

WOMAN: Oh God it's you! The Romford maggot! Get off your
  knees and take off that mask. You're not worthy of it. [*He does so*]
  Now cower behind my mother, it's easier when you're all together.

MOTHER: My word he's a handsome boy! What's he like in bed?

WOMAN: Mother! [*To CHIEF*] Would you like me to release you
  from the case?

CHIEF KIDNAPPER: Yes please!

WOMAN: Right Reverend, collect their weapons in this. [*Throws
  him a bag*]

PRIEST: Right you are!

MOTHER: Do you need a hand, my dear.

WOMAN: Yes, if you'd hold the case up for me...

CHIEF KIDNAPPER: What about taking these handcuffs off?

MOTHER: Shut up fishface!

WOMAN: [*Pointing gun at them*] Hold on while I switch the combination. [*Opens the case*] Right, back you lot.

CHIEF KIDNAPPER: It's here! It's not newspaper!

ALL: Hooray!

WOMAN: [*To CHIEF*] Get your hand out or I'll blow it off!

CHIEF KIDNAPPER: I just wanted to check they weren't fakes.

WOMAN: Mother is already taking care of that. What's the prog-
  nosis mother?

MOTHER: Real beauties, brand new! Let's see I'd say about... a
  million?

WOMAN: Well done mother, you've guessed the weight. Now you
  can put those notes back.

MOTHER: What notes?

WOMAN: The ones you whipped up your sleeve.

MOTHER: [*Aside, while putting the money back*] She always humili-
  ates me, even in front of strangers.

WOMAN: And the rest.

MOTHER: What rest?

WOMAN: Under your blouse.

MOTHER: My professional commission!
  [*She gives back the money. WOMAN closes the case*]

CHIEF KIDNAPPER: Why are you shutting it? What about divid-
  ing it up?

WOMAN: We need to come to some sort of agreement first.

CHIEF KIDNAPPER: OK, let's discuss it.

ALL: Yes let's discuss it.

[*All immediately sit cross-legged on the floor*]

WOMAN: Snook... Willoughby handed this over to you?

KIDNAPPERS: Yes.

WOMAN: Why?

CHIEF KIDNAPPER: That's what it said in your instructions!

WOMAN: Well, where is he now?

CHIEF KIDNAPPER: He said he was going back to the wine bar.

YOUNG MAN: The Gay Hussar!

WOMAN: So he isn't your boss?

KIDNAPPERS: No.

WOMAN: The lying insect! [*Opening fridge door*] Why did you tell me that Snookums...

KIDNAPPER 2: I was being burned alive, I had to say something.

WOMAN: Invertebrate!

CHIEF KIDNAPPER: Might I be released from this case?

WOMAN: No you may not! It's my insurance policy, you know what happens if you try to force the lock?

CHIEF KIDNAPPER: The whole thing explodes. A million quid up in smoke and one hand lost...

MOTHER: Diana you're a genius!

WOMAN: Right, let's get down to it. How much were you expecting to take home from this little caper?

CHIEF KIDNAPPER: Fifty...

KIDNAPPER 3: Forty...

KIDNAPPER 2: Thirty...

YOUNG MAN: Ten...

ALL: [*To the CHIEF*] You bastard!

CHIEF KIDNAPPER: We're on something of a sliding scale... [*Looking at KIDNAPPER 3*] Er... but, for the sake of solidarity, shall we say forty grand a piece.

KIDNAPPERS: Forty grand!

WOMAN: Remind me to talk about free collective bargaining. As long as I am supplied with all your photos plus exclusive rights, I am prepared to offer you twenty- five thousand each. Except the maggot, who'll be lucky to get the price of a single ticket to Romford.

KIDNAPPERS: Twenty-five grand!

YOUNG MAN: Two pounds eighty!

CHIEF KIDNAPPER: Alright, we'll settle for thirty...

WOMAN: Haggling is never successful when staring down the barrel of a shot-gun. Twenty-five, and that's being generous.

MOTHER: It's true, my daughter has always been generous, you know when she was thirteen...

WOMAN: Thank you Mother!

PRIEST: While we are on the sordid subject of money. I am presently collecting for the bell-tower, and I wondered whether one couldn't have a little something...

WOMAN: Vicar you should be ashamed of yourself. This is a kidnap ransom.

PRIEST: Well, [*Pointing at the shot gun*] I'm sure they could be persuaded to repent...

CHIEF KIDNAPPER: Look...

PRIEST: Then it's a clear conscience for them, clean money for me... us... the parish.

CHIEF KIDNAPPER: Who are you? A bloody evangelist?

WOMAN: Twenty-five thousand it is. However, I can offer an incentive bonus...

KIDNAPPERS: Yes!

WOMAN: Have you asked yourself why I came back?

KIDNAPPERS: No!

MOTHER: To save your mother...

WOMAN: Crap! No I came back to offer to double your money.

KIDNAPPERS: Fifty grand!

YOUNG MAN: Five pounds sixty!

MOTHER: Diana, you're off your head! [*Going to get gun out of bag*] Give me a gun I'll blast the lot of them.

WOMAN: [*Stopping her*] The extra twenty-five thousand will be handed out when you bring me here, nicely wrapped up, your boss.

KIDNAPPERS: What!

WOMAN: The boss... middle-man, insider, the organiser of my abduction.

CHIEF KIDNAPPER: We can't do that.

WOMAN: After all I've tried to teach you, you remain proletarian sheep, blindly obedient to your employer. It's ironic; the only workers with a sense of loyalty are criminals.

CHIEF KIDNAPPER: Oh no it isn't that, it's just...

PRIEST: Madam, you must rid yourself of this obsessive need for revenge. Forgive, turn the other cheek, be merciful... And think of the church bell-tower which is practically falling down.

WOMAN: Well try not to walk under it. So nobody's willing to give me the name. Well just to encourage you, let me inform you that I have all your names and addresses.

KIDNAPPER 3: She's like the old bill. "Better talk we know everything anyway".

WOMAN: OK! I'll call the register. Willie "The Flash" Dalton.

KIDNAPPER 2: Here miss! I mean, oh shit and bloody hell that's me.

WOMAN: Elvis "War-Zone" Birtwhistle.

KIDNAPPER 3: How the f...

WOMAN: And Rocky "The Bore" Walsingham-Smythe. [*To CHIEF*] I believe that's you. Now I just need the maggot's name, no-one seems to know...

KIDNAPPER 3: Alright, who squealed?

CHIEF KIDNAPPER: [*Looking at KIDNAPPER 2*] Well it's obvious, the ice man...

KIDNAPPER 3: You... [*He makes a gesture to KIDNAPPER 2 of starting up a chain-saw*]

KIDNAPPER 2: My fridge needs me. [*Shutting the door*]

WOMAN: You may as well take your masks off.

[*They do so*]

MOTHER: [*To CHIEF*] My God! It's my chiropodist.

PRIEST: Archbishop! [*Kissing KIDNAPPER 3's hand*] Your eminence.

KIDNAPPER 3: Get off! Woofta!

WOMAN: Will someone give me the bastard's name?

MOTHER: Diana! Don't give them a penny.

PRIEST: Listen to your mother, and invest it in the bell-tower.

MOTHER: If that money comes my way, I'll get you the name and address and family tree, in five seconds flat.

WOMAN: How?

MOTHER: I'll go into a trance... and summon a spirit to help us.

WOMAN: Stop talking nonsense, or you'll be in the fridge too!

KIDNAPPER 2: Oh no, I'm sorry! This is a private fridge. Privé!

MOTHER: Reverend, will you give me a hand.

[*MOTHER puts a chair on the table. PRIEST helps her on to it*]

CHIEF KIDNAPPER: To be honest, we'd more than willingly tell you his name, but we haven't got a clue ourselves. We've never actually seen him face to face.

WOMAN: How did he make the arrangements? By phone? Fax?

KIDNAPPER 3: No, we met him, [*Adopting hushed tones*] but he never turned up with the same face, he was disguised. Once, he had a pointed nose, bald head and blue eyes.

YOUNG MAN: When I saw him he was really fat with a potato nose and dreadlocks.

CHIEF KIDNAPPER: Another time he was dressed as the Queen Mother.

WOMAN: Who is this guy? Harry Enfield?

KIDNAPPER 3: But every time he would show us his calling card.

YOUNG MAN: Yeah! The bank note.

CHIEF KIDNAPPER: The Japanese bank note on water-marked paper dated 1888.

KIDNAPPER 3: He kept it in a tin.

YOUNG MAN: A silver tin.

[*It has all become very intimate and hushed but the atmosphere is broken by the MOTHER chanting*]

MOTHER: [*Mumbling*] *Ana tros perkeious yunii banagonis...*

WOMAN: What's she doing?

PRIEST: She's talking ancient Greek.

WOMAN: She can't be! She doesn't even know the modern sort. She's making it up.

PRIEST: Show some respect! Come on now boys, give me a hand with this table .

[*KIDNAPPERS help him carry MOTHER, table and chair to the centre of the room*]

WOMAN: Don't encourage her!

PRIEST: Be at peace, oh anguished soul. Tell us who you are.

MOTHER: *Main y ack e itriost cyc o pathy omer god mer darus...*

WOMAN: What did she say?

PRIEST: [*To MOTHER*] *At i win do wus or sea ling us a buv ous...*

MOTHER: *Sea Lingus.*

PRIEST: [*Crouching under the table*] She has found a spirit with knowledge of this place and the people in it.

YOUNG MAN: I wonder who it is?

WOMAN: Oh come on mother! While you're about it why not ask what really happened to Robert Maxwell and was Elvis a junkie...

PRIEST: Come now, don't provoke the spirits.

MOTHER: *Traimes exte reem lea aro gant beech...*

PRIEST: And seeing ye are without faith...

MOTHER: *Sheeta brickus a bee gus sur preesus...*

PRIEST: I will reveal myself.

[*Lights off sound of rapid gun fire*]

[*Lights back on*]

KIDNAPPER 3: They've sent in the army!

YOUNG MAN: It's the mass-murderer! She's called up the spirit who haunts this place the one with the sawn-off shot gun. The witch has summoned him...

KIDNAPPER 3: What do we do ?

CHIEF KIDNAPPER: I resign!

WOMAN: This is ridiculous! Spirits don't fire real bullets.

[*Lights out, rapid gun fire and a loud noise*]

[*Lights on*]

KIDNAPPER 2: She's the Devil's mother, we're all about to burn in hell.

YOUNG MAN: The room seems smaller somehow.

CHIEF KIDNAPPER: It's just an illusion.

[*Loud rumbling*]

PRIEST: [*To MOTHER*] *Exapi rapidus...*

MOTHER: *Attandi constrictus commus sardinus...*

WOMAN: What's she dribbling on about?

MOTHER: *Illegitimus Masamiba!*

PRIEST: That I really cannot translate. Everybody out!

CHIEF KIDNAPPER: Everybody out!

KIDNAPPER 3: [*At top of stairs*] This door's locked!

YOUNG MAN: [*At kitchen door*] So's this one!

CHIEF KIDNAPPER: Shit!

KIDNAPPER 2: "Guide me O thou great Jehov..."

ALL: Shut up!

[*More rumbling and the walls start to move in*]

PRIEST: Look the walls are coming in.

KIDNAPPER 3: He's right we're going to be condensed.

WOMAN: It must be an illusion.

CHIEF KIDNAPPER: It's an illusion!

PRIEST: Your mother has exorcised something diabolical. Only she can save us now. [*To MOTHER*] *Exapi, exapi ten ereef...*

MOTHER: *Exapi panama!*

YOUNG MAN: It may be just an illusion but the walls are moving.

[*Walls continue to move in. Everyone is gathering on or around table*]

WOMAN: Mother, stop it!

CHIEF KIDNAPPER: Help!

KIDNAPPER 3: We could shoot the walls back.

KIDNAPPER 2: Repent! Prepare to meet thy maker.

PRIEST: That's my line.

WOMAN: Don't push.

KIDNAPPER 3: It's not me, it's the wall

WOMAN: It's not the wall hanging on to my tits.

KIDNAPPER 3: Just getting my balance.

WOMAN: Mother come down from there.

MOTHER: [*Sharply*] I'm in a trance! Infidel! [*Going for it*] *Pantheon acropolis demis rososs cromenos elgin marbelus...*

[*Everybody is climbing on everyone else trying to get on the table*]

CHIEF KIDNAPPER: Vicar, you're standing on my head.

WOMAN: Who's playing with my bottom?

YOUNG MAN: Sorry! It's my thurible... It's stuck!

KIDNAPPER 2: Don't drink the nectar, it tastes like shit!

YOUNG MAN: Diana, can't we be friends, kiss and make-up?

WOMAN: Get away from me! Remove your thurible from my bottom. Mother, what's going... [*She collapses*]

CHIEF KIDNAPPER: Keep that thurible away from this case.

MOTHER: Don't push now, please! Hand me that gun.

KIDNAPPER 3: I said we should shoot the walls back.

MOTHER: I'm not going to shoot it, I'm going to play it! [*She lifts the barrel to her mouth, blows it and a sound like a horn comes out*]

PRIEST: Look the walls are receding!

CHIEF KIDNAPPER: It's incredible!

YOUNG MAN: It's a miracle!

CHIEF KIDNAPPER: Well done mother!

KIDNAPPER 2: I told you she was a witch.

PRIEST: Look your daughter's lost her senses.

CHIEF KIDNAPPER: Someone wake her up, we need the combination for the case.

MOTHER: Wake her up hell, I know the combination. Give me a hand tying her up.

KIDNAPPER 3: Leave it to me. [*Starts tying her up*]

YOUNG MAN: I'll help! [*Does so*]

KIDNAPPER 2: Don't forget the alcohol and the electrodes.

CHIEF KIDNAPPER: Why are you tying up your daughter?

MOTHER: Because she's out for the count.

CHIEF KIDNAPPER: Oh I see.

MOTHER: Right, do you want that ransom or not?

KIDNAPPER 3: Course we do!

MOTHER: [*Holds up syringe*] Who can give my daughter an injection?

KIDNAPPER 2: Me!

YOUNG MAN: I will!

KIDNAPPER 3: Give it here! [*Takes syringe, and injects WOMAN*]

MOTHER: When you've topped her up, gag her and put her in the next room.

KIDNAPPER 2: We could put her in the fridge, it's lovely in there.

CHIEF KIDNAPPER: So she didn't pass out! You drugged her.

MOTHER: In the top draw next to the sink you'll find the key to that door, drag her in and lock the door.

CHIEF KIDNAPPER: How do you know where everything is? I don't understand any of this, the shots, the walls start coming in, our hostage is knocked out by her own mother who then gets her tied up, locked in and starts taking over...

KIDNAPPER 2: It's the sort of thing you expect from the ruling classes.

CHIEF KIDNAPPER: [*To MOTHER*] What gives you the right to order us about?

MOTHER: Well, there's this! [*Points shot-gun at them*] And this! [*Holds up bank note*]

CHIEF KIDNAPPER: My God! It's the...

KIDNAPPERS: 1888 Japanese yen.

CHIEF KIDNAPPER: You're the boss!

YOUNG MAN: The middleman, the insider, the organiser, the exploit...

KIDNAPPER 3: Bloody hell!

CHIEF KIDNAPPER: We helped the Mother to kidnap her own daughter.

KIDNAPPER 2: Told you! That's what you expect from the ruling classes!

CHIEF KIDNAPPER: And you were the master of disguise?

MOTHER: No, that was a colleague of mine. [*Hands gun to PRIEST*]

CHIEF KIDNAPPER: So you know the combination for this lock?

MOTHER: Yes!

CHIEF KIDNAPPER: Well, would you mind freeing my wrist?

KIDNAPPER 3: [*Grabbing MOTHER from behind*] Got her! I'll knock her out too.

CHIEF KIDNAPPER: No, you cretin, she's got to release me first. [*Moving in on MOTHER*] Alright, Witch, you better release me or he's going to...

PRIEST: Get away from the lady or we'll shoot.

YOUNG MAN: We?

PRIEST: If you look immediately above your heads you'll see a small hole in the ceiling through which the barrel of a shot gun is protruding.

KIDNAPPER 2: Oh yes, he's right, look.

PRIEST: Meet Rupert, my altar boy.

KIDNAPPER 2: Hullo Rupert!

YOUNG MAN: There's another hole right next to it look!

MOTHER: That's the video camera. If anyone's going to sell the story of this kidnapping it's going to be me.

CHIEF KIDNAPPER: I don't believe it! Gun-toting clergy.

KIDNAPPER 2: Well that's what you expect in the modern parish!

KIDNAPPER 3: Don't get over-excited Your Reverence.

MOTHER: Thank you, Reverend!

PRIEST: You won't forget my bell-tower?

MOTHER: How could I! [*To CHIEF*] Come here and I'll free you... don't try anything clever we've got you covered. How lovely! It's just like the pictures. You lot really are the most incompetent bunch. You'd think after all this time with my daughter you'd have learned something about crime. [*Releasing CHIEF*] Now get back while I hand out the dosh. How much are you due then?

CHIEF KIDNAPPER: Well, we have been offered fifty thousand a head.

MOTHER: But that was only if you told her the name of the boss. But I'm the boss and I revealed myself so that twenty-five grand reward goes to me.

KIDNAPPER 2: That's what you expect from capitalists!

CHIEF KIDNAPPER: It's not fair, we deserve a loyalty bonus.

MOTHER: Didn't anyone ever tell you not to negotiate with someone holding a gun?

KIDNAPPER 2: Yes! As a matter of...

YOUNG MAN: Can I just say that I think two pounds twenty is...

MOTHER: Don't worry I operate a fair pay scheme.

CHIEF KIDNAPPER: So it's twenty-five grand each.

YOUNG MAN: Twenty-five grand!

MOTHER: Right, twenty-five - but gross.

KIDNAPPER 3: You mean we're on PAYE?

MOTHER: I have to take off my expenses, renting this place, the mobile walls, which worked to perfection, equipment, business lunches etc. [*Gets out a calculator*]

CHIEF KIDNAPPER: We were warned about this bit.

KIDNAPPER 3: Bastard mothers!

KIDNAPPER 2: That's what people like us must expect from the ruling classes!

YOUNG MAN: Twenty-five grand!

MOTHER: Here is the final amount three thousand three hundred and fifty pounds.

KIDNAPPERS: Three thousand three hundred and fifty pounds!

CHIEF KIDNAPPER: What a rip-off.

MOTHER: Reverend would you mind distributing their wages. You may as well round up to three thousand.

PRIEST: Alright!

CHIEF KIDNAPPER: What are we to do with your daughter?

MOTHER: Ah! I'll leave her with you to keep her out of circulation for a few days.

KIDNAPPER 2: How many days?

MOTHER: Seven.

KIDNAPPER 2: Right I'm going back to my fridge.

CHIEF KIDNAPPER: [*To KIDNAPPER 2*] You stay there! [*To MOTHER*] We have to look after your daughter for seven days?

MOTHER: You get an extra three grand each for one weeks work.

CHIEF KIDNAPPER: Three grand for a week with your daughter...

KIDNAPPERS: Forget it!

MOTHER: You could keep her unconscious...

CHIEF KIDNAPPER: Ten grand!

MOTHER: Five.

CHIEF KIDNAPPER: Nine?

MOTHER: Alright seven!

KIDNAPPERS: Done!

MOTHER: Give them ten grand vicar.

PRIEST: Delighted, there's nothing I wouldn't do for my bell-tower! Incidentally I have something of a problem with the vestry too...

MOTHER: No!

PRIEST: Forget I mentioned it.

MOTHER: [*To CHIEF*] Take a look at this. [*Handing him map*] [*To KIDNAPPER 3*] And you go and fetch my daughter and if she looks like she's coming round give her a jab.

CHIEF KIDNAPPER: It's a map!

MOTHER: My you're a bright boy! It's another safe house for you to move to, there's a car outside, put her in it and off you go.

CHIEF KIDNAPPER: Well, it looks like we're on the move.

[*KIDNAPPER 3 enters carrying body over his shoulder*]

MOTHER: And don't put that fridge cretin on guard this time.

KIDNAPPER 2: Witch!

[*They start up the stairs as DIANA appears at the top with shot-gun*]

KIDNAPPER 3: Fuck me rigid!

CHIEF KIDNAPPER: It's another McKaye!

DIANA: No! Not another McKaye but the real McKaye!

YOUNG MAN: So that one is the double.

KIDNAPPER 3: [*Dropping the body he is carrying*] I knew it!

KIDNAPPER 2: I've been flambé-ed by an actress.

MOTHER: Oh bollocks!

DIANA: I must admit she was superb.

MOTHER: These sodding glasses!

DIANA: Never mind the glasses, mother! Aren't you ashamed of yourself abducting your own daughter... to sell her for a million pounds?

MOTHER: I needed the money. You allow me a pittance. What's the good of having a millionaire daughter if I have to spend my last few years cutting out coupons from the paper and waiting for meals on wheels. And then, my dear daughter, an extraordinary thing has happened: I've fallen in love.

DIANA: Yes I know, and you intended to escape to South America with him.

MOTHER: How did you know?

DIANA: First, mother, your house is bugged from top to bottom...

MOTHER: Bugged! So that's why the Azalea was picking up GLR!

DIANA: Secondly, I had Justin infiltrated in to the gang...

CHORUS: Justin?

DIANA: Yes. The maggot...

CHORUS: Kevin?

YOUNG MAN: Turncoat at your service!

CHORUS: Bastard!

KIDNAPPER 2: As I've said before, that's what you expect...

CHIEF KIDNAPPER: So our traitor was really your traitor.

YOUNG MAN: Oh I believe this is yours Di! [*Produces ruby ring*]

DIANA: Isn't he a darling? It's no good looking up to the heavens, mother, I have disarmed the angelic altar boy and he is currently crushing insects in the blending room. Now, the only thing I haven't found out is - who's your lover is?

MOTHER: You'll never guess!

DIANA: Justin darling, relieve the priest of his weapon. Now, Father there's something familiar about you. [*Going up to him*]

PRIEST: Madam please! Have respect for my cloth.

DIANA: Ah a wig, and a false nose. Good lord Charlie, that's incredible!

MOTHER: Yes, Diana it's your husband Charles Forbes-McKaye.

KIDNAPPER 2: Personally, I'm not the least bit surprised.

DIANA: But what are you doing disguised like that?

PRIEST: I was helping out.

DIANA: So you are the missing link!

CHIEF KIDNAPPER: Harry Enfield!

KIDNAPPER 3: The middle-man!

KIDNAPPER 2: The estate agent!!!

KIDNAPPER 3: We were kidnapping her for her mother and her husband.

KIDNAPPER 2: Standard practice for the ruling classes.

DIANA: The pair of you got together to clean me out.

PRIEST: You despised me... Treated me like an idiot...

DIANA: You are an idiot!

PRIEST: Humiliated me, abused me and now I found someone who values and loves me.

DIANA: You mean my mother?

PRIEST: She's an adorable woman.

KIDNAPPER 3: She's a witch!

DIANA: Charlie, you've fallen in love with my mother?

KIDNAPPER 2: Ah so that's the bell-tower he wanted to restore!

MOTHER: Diana your husband loves me!

PRIEST: Yes, I love your mother!

KIDNAPPER 2: That's what we've come to expect from the aristocracy!

DIANA: Let's get on with the *coup de grace*. [*To KIDNAPPERS*] You can give me back the ten thousands.

CHORUS: That's our salary.

KIDNAPPER 2: See how the rich and powerful fight among themselves and we're the ones who suffer.

YOUNG MAN: Shut up! [*To PRIEST*] Alright Charlie hand over the readies.

DIANA: That's my bit of rough.

PRIEST: What about South America?

DIANA: Well I have got a little surprise for you. [*To YOUNG MAN*] Take the money out. I'm going to leave the case for you.

CHORUS: What, empty!

DIANA: Not quite, you're forgetting the layer of TNT.

CHORUS: Bloody hell!

[*YOUNG MAN hangs case from ceiling*]

DIANA: From the instant we trip the mechanism, there will be exactly thirty seconds to the explosion. OK Justin.

MOTHER: Diana! You can't kill your own mother?

DIANA: You taught me everything I know! There's no-one more criminal than you. Twenty six!

PRIEST: And your husband?

DIANA: Except my husband. Twenty four!

CHIEF KIDNAPPER: Your secretary? She risked her life for you.

DIANA: It'll teach her to seduce young men in my meat... er apartment. Nineteen!

KIDNAPPER 2: What about us, workers, pawns...

CHORUS: Yes, what about us!

DIANA: You deserve to be blown up, it's an important lesson, that's...

CHORUS: What you have to expect from the ruling classes.

YOUNG MAN: [*Exiting*] Diana, twelve seconds, let's go!

DIANA: Farewell losers!

CHORUS: 9,8,7,6,5,4,3,2,1, aaaahhhh!

DIANA: Sorry audience! I can't allow it to end like this. Wouldn't look good! The rich heiress, who set up the whole thing, getting away scot free with all the money, having blown up everyone else. What would the media make of that! The rich caricatured as a bunch of ruthless, exploitative, cynical, criminal matricides.

[*YOUNG MAN re-enters with video camera*]

Good you've got it! The camera would be best over there. Lot's of close ups on me. Now then, as much sincerity as you can manage. Mother take it again from your line and... action.

MOTHER: Diana, your husband loves me!

PRIEST: Yes, I love your mother!

DIANA: Mother, husband, how pleased I am to see you both happy. I, who have always treated you with such shabby contempt. I could weep.